NATIONAL INSTITUTE SOC
NO.

GW01081204

SOCIAL WORK IN GENERAL PRACTICE

SOCIAL WORK
IN GENERAL PRACTICE

by

E. MATILDA GOLDBERG

and

JUNE E. NEILL

Tilde 0144 284 33?9

London
GEORGE ALLEN & UNWIN LIMITED
RUSKIN HOUSE   MUSEUM STREET

n/r Dur brist new

ISBN 0 04 360025 5 hardback
0 04 360026 3 paper

Printed in Great Britain
in 11 point *Fournier type*
by Unwin Brothers Limited, Woking and London

CAVERSHAM PROJECT CONSULTATIVE COMMITTEE

Dame Eileen Younghusband, DBE (Chairman)
Dr Hugh Faulkner
Dr Wilfred G. Harding
Mr John S. Heap
Mr Robin Huws Jones, CBE
Professor Robert F. L. Logan
Miss Alice M. Sheridan

PRACTICE STAFF

Dr Hugh C. Faulkner	Senior Partner
Mrs Lavender Aaronovitch	Social Worker's Secretary
Dr David J. Boulton	Trainee General Practitioner
Dr Margaret Gilchrist	General Practitioner
Mrs Elsie Gollan	Administrative Secretary
Dr Donald M. Grant	General Practitioner
Mrs Elizabeth Hall	Senior Receptionist
Dr Ruth D'Arcy Hart	Family Planning and Marital Problems
Miss Joyce Jameson	Health Visitor
Mrs Tina Levins	Secretary/Receptionist
Dr Rachel Miller	General Practitioner
Mrs Barbara Patterson	Health Visitor
Dr Allan H. Pote	General Practitioner
Dr Peter A. M. Raine	Trainee General Practitioner
Miss Rosemary Wadsworth	Community Service Volunteer
Miss Marian Weiss	Practice Sister
Mrs Ami Yureth	Health Visitor

FOREWORD

This book records a five year project to explore the contribution of social work in general practice. It was undertaken jointly by the Caversham Group Practice Team and the National Institute for Social Work Training and financed by the City Parochial Foundation. Although the idea was not new, the Caversham Project is perhaps the most systematic attempt so far to study in action the contribution a social worker can make to the identification and treatment of psychosocial problems in general practice. It also attempts to clarify the elements in the partnership between doctors and social workers.

What later became the Caversham Project arose from a chance meeting between us at a Royal Society of Health Conference in 1960. Although the idea was kept alive, the means were lacking until Sir Donald Allen, at that time Clerk to the City Parochial Foundation, immediately saw its possibilities. Robin Huws Jones, then Principal of the National Institute for Social Work Training, agreed that it could clarify some debated issues about the nature and effectiveness of social work, interdisciplinary co-operation and good 'pick-up' points for the deployment of social workers.

A Consultative Committee was set up, the post was advertised and it was decided to appoint the best applicant without regard to the particular field of casework in which he or she had practised. Miss June Neill, a family caseworker, was appointed and amply demonstrated that the quality of casework and the ability to work as a member of a team are more important than previous experience in a particular setting. At the same time, the monitoring and analysis of this demonstration owe a great deal to the distinguished contribution made by Miss E. M. Goldberg, who came to the National Institute for Social Work Training as Director of Research from the Social Medicine Unit of the Medical Research Council when the experiment was just starting. We were fortunate also in that the initiative had come from a general practice which saw the need for a social work member of the team, rather than from outsiders. By his active interest, Dr. Wilfrid Harding, Medical Officer of Health for the London Borough of Camden made an important contribution to the effectiveness of the project. The Consultative Committee also performed a useful function as a sounding board of medical and social work opinion.

We are not primarily concerned here to pay tribute to the people who contributed, however richly this is deserved. Rather we want to identify the attitudes and climate which seem essential if pioneer demonstration projects in interdisciplinary co-operation—in this instance between general practice and social work—are to be successfully conducted. In the current jargon, where roles are not yet institutionalised there must be a good deal of professional candour, curiosity and a willingness to learn from each other and to discover what constitutes the best milieu for co-operation so that the most effective 'rules, roles and relationships' can be evolved for more general application.

From another angle, this demonstration owes its origin to changes in the whole concept of general practice or primary medical care, from the relatively simple ideas of organic pathology, to awareness of the complex and interrelated emotional, social and economic causes of patients' needs. At this earlier period very little of the academic training of doctors or their hospital practice had any relevance to the stream of undifferentiated demand they met in general practice. They found themselves expected to deliver instant wisdom in response to infinitely wide-ranging demand—a sitting duck every morning and evening. General practitioners were already, however, being pressed to predict vulnerability, to diagnose reversible pathology early enough for something to be done. Patients were demanding aid with emotional and psychological problems—however much they cloaked their cry for help in acceptable physical symptoms. Doctors began to feel that they should try to equip themselves to respond, or else ask whether other professionals (and non-professionals) might respond, not just as well as, but demonstrably better than they could themselves. This led many doctors to believe that the future depended on re-educating themselves—in preventive medicine, earlier diagnosis, emotional illness, rehabilitation and so on. At the same time they were increasingly asking other workers—nurses, health visitors, social workers, receptionists and secretaries—to join them in the primary care team in group practices and health centres, working closely with their colleagues in the hospitals and the community health and welfare services.

Social casework also had to advance to the point where communication and 'dovetailing' co-operation with a general practice team became practicable. This demanded respect by each profession for the others—a willingness to work out a common language for communication and to accept the different tempo of medical and social work interviews. To achieve this the social worker must be a good and articulate practitioner in his or her own right, understanding the content and boundaries of professional social work competence and must be seen to be making a useful contribution, both by doctors and patients. In the Caversham Project, as elsewhere, this proved to have two aspects: first the social worker's ability to assess the psycho-social components in the troubles of patients referred by the doctors. Assessment sometimes led to crisis intervention or to short—and occasionally longer—term treatment. A second aspect was knowledge of the social services and how to use them in combination and in ways acceptable to patients to meet their specific needs. But even in a borough as well supplied with services as Camden, it transpired that over half the patients referred to the social worker had not apparently been in touch with any other social service agency.

It is good to report that, thanks to the continued support of the City Parochial Foundation, the Caversham Project has led to a further demonstration in which the main responsibility is carried by the Health and Social Services Departments of the London Borough of Camden. A social worker is now co-operating with both the Caversham and the James Wigg Centres, which will shortly be housed in the Kentish Town Health Centre, a teaching health centre closely linked with University College Hospital.

Our project was completed before the local authority social services departments came into existence. These comprehensive services can all the better use the excellent pick-up point which a general practice team provides, with its continuing relation to patients unselected in terms of age, sex and class—to quote the Seebohm Report 'In other words, everybody'.

HUGH FAULKNER,   EILEEN YOUNGHUSBAND
General Practitioner,   *Chairman, Caversham Project*
Caversham Centre   *Consultative Committee*

CONTENTS

ACKNOWLEDGEMENTS

So many people have contributed to this project and to the completion of the report that it is not possible to mention everyone by name.

The City Parochial Foundation financed the study and we thank them for their generous grant and for the interest they have always shown in our work.

Dame Eileen Younghusband together with Dr Hugh Faulkner formulated this project and translated the idea into reality; we have benefited not only from this but also from her skill as Chairman of the Consultative Committee, and we thank her for the careful attention she has always paid to our requests for help, advice and comment. The Consultative Committee gave freely of their specialist knowledge, which was particularly valuable during the first years of the project when ideas and plans were being formulated.

The support for the project by Dr W. Harding, Camden's Medical Officer of Health, exerted an important influence on the ready co-operation we enjoyed from many people working in the Borough services.

The Caversham project would not have come into existence without the personality and leadership of Dr Hugh Faulkner, senior partner of the Caversham Centre group practice team. Working as a member of his team has been a stimulating and precious experience.

Dr Mary Speak, formerly Statistician at the National Institute for Social Work Training, helped us to design the record card and supervised the first computer analysis. Her successor Dr David Fruin undertook with patience and good humour the demanding task of completing and checking the statistical analysis of the data. Much work was carried out on the statistical data by our research assistants Mrs Elizabeth Morton and Miss Christine Marynowicz. Mrs Doris Kent and Mrs Ruby Woodward spent many weary hours producing additional data by hand.

We were greatly helped by detailed comments made on the final draft by Miss Inge Bergman, Dr Ann Cartwright, Professor Margot Jefferys and Dame Eileen Younghusband. We have been greatly encouraged by the interest and support of the officers of the Department of Health and Social Security.

It is difficult to convey how much we owe to Mr Robin Huws Jones, Principal of the National Institute for Social Work Training, who did meticulous work not only on the final, but also on the preceding, drafts. We thank him for this, but most of all for the wise, kind and consistent support he has always given.

Secretarial help during the field-work phase was given by Mrs Lavender Aaronovitch, and we are grateful to her not only for her unvarying reliability and versatility but also for the loyalty and warmth she showed to the social worker and the patients alike. Her sense of humour was a great asset.

Miss Linda Climpson typed many of the earlier drafts of the report and other secretaries of the National Institute for Social Work Training have given us additional help. We thank them all for their patience, and especially Mrs Pitman, who often came to our rescue in a secretarial emergency.

We are also much indebted to Mrs Maureen Webley, librarian at the Institute, for her enthusiastic pursuit of the pertinent literature.

Throughout this project we have met many general practitioners, health visitors and social workers who have encouraged us by their lively interest and discussions. We hope that they will find something in this report which will help them to develop the fruitful ideas generated by them and others about the inter-related roles of general practice and social work.

E. M. G.
J. N.
1971

PART I

THE BACKGROUND

I

GENERAL PRACTICE AND SOCIAL WORK

Long before social workers came into being, patients consulted their doctors not only about physical illness but about their social and emotional problems. Until comparatively recent times most of the medicines dispensed had few pharmocologically curative properties, hence psycho-social remedies must have been a vital ingredient of the physician's art. But the social or emotional malaise underlying physical complaints often went unrecognised by either patient or doctor.

The steady advances during this century in the behavioural sciences, in psychiatry and in social medicine have helped to define the social and emotional factors in illness and to fashion treatment tools; though much is still unknown. At the same time, the increase in rising expectations strengthened the patients' demands for the treatment of psycho-social ills. Patients were no longer prepared to put up with marital unhappiness, damaging housing conditions, general depression and anxiety, as inevitable burdens, and they began to look to their doctors and other helping professions for relief, if not for cure. By now it is commonly accepted that a considerable proportion of the undifferentiated complaints which general practitioners encounter are mainly of a psycho-social nature, requiring for their treatment knowledge of social resources, as well as social and psychological skills. For example, a random sample of general practitioners in Buckinghamshire thought that about a third of the patients they saw in a typical day's work had social or psychological problems which impeded their daily activities or social relationships (Jefferys, 1965).

In 1965 Professor R. Scott, who pioneered the idea of introducing a social worker into the general practice team, put the problem this way:

'... the aetiology of much of the disease we encounter in general practice, and many of the factors which complicate our management of the sick person, have their origins in social maladjustment and in inadequate or faulty interpersonal relationships. To the extent that this is so our therapy

B

will become less concerned with manipulating the patient's blood chemistry and more preoccupied with the physical, economic and social factors in the patient's environment. The decision which is taken as to whether such problems will be regarded as the sole responsibility of the medical profession or the exclusive concern of society or as a field which requires a full partnership between medicine and other related social agencies, will be a major factor in determining the future of general practice.' (Scott, 1965).

Since then a succession of official reports has sought to clarify the functions of the modern general practitioner, both in relation to the medical profession as a whole and in relation to other helping professions. The report of the Royal Commission on Medical Education (1968) saw the general practitioner of the future as a 'primary physician' of very broad competence and interests, much better acquainted with the behavioural sciences, community medicine and psychiatry than his predecessor. The report forecasts 'a gradually increasing delegation of a variety of tasks from the qualified doctor to colleagues in other professions'. Problems are foreseen in defining the kind of non-medical staff 'who can usefully contribute to the work of a medical practice'. The suggestion is made that 'something more than the traditional skills and qualities of nurses and social workers will be required', but the report does not define these additional skills.

The recent reports of the working party of the British Medical Association Planning Unit on Primary Medical Care (1970) and the report of the Royal College of General Practitioners (1970) have stressed once more the generality of general practice and its substantial concern with social pathology. They suggest that the behavioural sciences have much to contribute to the knowledge-base of the general practitioner whose work will increasingly involve the care of patients with degenerative diseases of middle life, chronic and multiple infirmities of old age and problems of a psycho-social nature, as well as childhood illnesses. The report on Primary Medical Care envisages that

'the clinical skills of the primary physician should enable him not so much to attach a diagnostic label, as to unravel the undifferentiated clinical problem which is often a complex of physical, emotional and social factors and to take or initiate appropriate action. Skills should also include the capacity to work harmoniously as a member of the team.'

This concept of teamwork, sharing the work with other helpers belonging to different disciplines, contrasts with the old notion of the exclusive, if not possessive, personal relationship between the general practitioner and his patient.

Teamwork between doctors, social workers and other specialists was to be the cornerstone of the health centres envisaged in the National Health Services Act of 1947, but, as is well known, this idea did not catch on among general practitioners and hardly any health centres came into being in the fifties. The few which did—for example, Woodberry Down in North London—did not function with integrated teams, but merely provided common premises in which general practitioners, health visitors, infant welfare and child guidance clinics were located. Gradually, however, general practitioners themselves discovered the advantages of coming together in group practices. They enabled them to work more efficiently by pooling resources, and to give their patients more comprehensive care by employing ancillary staff, such as receptionists, nurses and recently, health visitors. Indeed, some group practices—such as the Caversham Centre, where the project described in this book took place—became little nuclei of health centres. By the middle sixties the concept of health centres staffed by multi-disciplinary teams began to gather momentum among forward-looking general practitioners; at the time of writing, 167 health centres are in existence and a further 189 have been approved by the Department of Health and Social Security. (HMSO 1971.)

There have been heated discussions about the threat that teamwork presents to the confidential doctor-patient relationship. But did this close relationship ever exist for the mass of working-class patients? It is also worth noting that in child guidance and adult psychiatry, both of which deal with very personal and emotionally highly sensitive areas of people's lives, teamwork often enhances the understanding of patients' problems. It makes their care more differentiated and comprehensive, without losing the personal touch or sacrificing confidentiality.

Despite doubts among some general practitioners, teamwork in general practice is growing, particularly in relation to community nursing. Anderson and his colleagues reported (1970) that the percentages of general practices with attachments of community nurses rose from 11 to 24 per cent in two years. The inclusion of social workers in the general practice team has been much slower to develop, although the idea goes back more than twenty years, when an almoner joined Dr Scott's group practice in Edinburgh (Patterson 1949). In the fifties Backett and his team, after studying a small rural practice

in Northern Ireland, concluded that 12 per cent of the families needed
social work help (Backett et al. 1957), and several experiments have
taken place since Dr Scott's pioneering demonstration (Dongray 1962,
Collins 1965, Dickinson and Harper 1968, Forman and Fairbairn 1968,
Ratoff and Pearson 1970, Cooper 1971). These projects range from
part-time secondment of specialist social workers, to the attachment
of a full-time social worker to a practice over several years. All these
social workers have found plenty of work in three capacities: as
assessors of social difficulties, as links and co-ordinators with social
services and as therapists. Recently Cooper has suggested a fourth
function: that of helping to secure the patient's co-operation in
medical care. The projects indicate that one full-time social worker
in a group practice of 9,000 to 10,0co patients can barely cope with
the needs arising, once the doctors have become aware of them and
of the possibilities of help.

Some enthusiastic general practitioners and notably Forman (Forman
and Fairbairn 1968) see general practice as the most promising community base for the development of social work. However, recent
studies in London, Birmingham and York reveal clearly that social
work remains largely an unknown quantity to general practitioners. A
survey of all general practitioners in one London borough (Harwin
et al. 1970), showed that few of the practitioners have regular or
frequent contact with any social agency and that the majority do not
feel the need for such contact. Of the interviewed doctors, 14 per cent
expressed definite interest in the possibility of a social worker attachment and a further 27 per cent welcomed the idea of regular meetings
and case discussions with a social worker, but a third firmly rejected
the notion of teamwork. In a survey carried out among Birmingham
general practitioners (McCulloch and Brown 1969) the majority (62
per cent) of doctors preferred a nursing background for social
workers and saw the social workers' functions as mainly concerned
with concrete and practical tasks, rather than with psychological help.
Only about a quarter of the general practitioners welcomed a new,
well-organised local authority social work department, outside the
control of a medical man. An inquiry into the use which general
practitioners in York made of mental welfare officers and psychiatric social workers in the community-care of their psychiatric patients,
indicated that general practitioners were not sure of the psychiatric
social workers' functions and that few had any sustained contact
with them, although the social workers were freely available at a
mental health centre. The high turnover of the social workers

seems to have contributed to this situation, as has the social workers' inability to communicate the nature of their skills to the general practitioners.

On the other hand, the rapid growth of the Derby scheme of social worker attachments to general practices, following initial apathy or even hostility, suggests that the general practitioners were converted to the idea of medico-social teamwork by example rather than precept (Cooper 1971).

The Seebohm Report (1968), which forms the blueprint for the reorganisation of the local authority personal social services, discusses the reasons for the poor collaboration between doctors and social workers when both are so dependent on communication and so involved in a common concern. The authors of the report suggest that the complexity of the social services, or sometimes the lack of them, can put off the keenest family doctor, and they refer also to the 'pre-occupation of some social workers with psycho-dynamics, often formidably expressed which may not be what a harassed family doctor or the situation self-evidently requires'. The report sees the more fundamental sources of difference between medicine and social work in the contrasting developments of the two professions. The social workers' emphasis, as the members of the Seebohm Committee saw it, is on patients gaining understanding of their situation and on the acquisition of personal insight and empathy on the part of social workers. Medicine, on the other hand, is concerned with refining its objectivity and technology. The authors argue that these two approaches are 'as different as they are obviously complementary'. The assumption that the doctor must always be the leader in any team of which he is a member was thought to be another factor in poor collaboration. The report refers to the need for social workers to learn more about the doctor's job and about advances and problems of medicine today. It also implicitly criticises the social workers' comparative lack of interest in evaluating the results of their work. The authors state unequivocably that they regard teamwork between general practitioners and the social services as vital, and suggest that health centres would provide a proper base for joint working. They recommend that social service departments should make a determined effort to collaborate with local general practitioners, that a variety of experiments in teamwork should be started and that as soon as doctors in a health centre or a sizeable group practice feel that they want the help of a social worker from the social service department, the department should do everything possible to meet such a request.

These quotations from the Seebohm Report which plead so forcibly for the closest collaboration between social work and medicine, contrast oddly with the cries of consternation that have arisen in the medical profession about the disservice this report and the reorganisation of the personal social services have done to the welfare of patients, by separating social service from medicine. If the project described in this book shows anything at all, it is the great difficulties and barriers to close collaboration which the fragmentation of the social services presented to the general practice team. And this applied whether the social worker was working in the health department of the local authority or elsewhere. All the members of the Caversham team were eargerly looking forward to the days when they no longer would have to adapt their patients' multiple needs to the special eligibility requirements of the different social services and when there would be one relevant area-office with which they could work and one telephone number to ring.

The Seebohm Committee wished they could have recommended the attachment of full-time social workers to all health centres and group practices, but they felt that not only was there a scarcity of social workers, but general practice was not yet ready for such a programme and more knowledge was needed about how doctors and social workers could most usefully collaborate.

This very theme formed the basis of the Caversham project which came into being through the convergence of two quests—the long-standing desire of the senior partner of the Caversham group practice, Dr Hugh Faulkner, to include a social worker in his team of doctor, nurse and health visitor, and the pioneering spirit of Dame Eileen Younghusband, who was searching for a general practice that would welcome the help of a social worker and one where her usefulness could be carefully explored and studied. Dame Eileen and some of her colleagues at the National Institute for Social Work Training began to discuss possibilities with the doctors of the Caversham Centre and the broad outlines of a joint enterprise emerged. The City Parochial Foundation was approached for a grant to support a five-year project; they responded generously and throughout maintained a keen and encouraging interest. Advertisements for a social worker produced an excellent field of candidates and Miss June Neill was appointed to the staff of the National Institute. For the following four years she was attached full-time to the Caversham group practice. Miss Goldberg became the consultant on both the casework and the monitoring and research aspects of the project. Well before the start of social work a meeting was held with key personnel of the Borough's health and welfare services, in which the developments leading to the project were outlined along with its aims. Comments and suggestions were invited, and boundaries and functions clarified, as far as this was possible at such an early stage.

The questions it was hoped to explore in the Caversham project were broadly these: What is the nature and range of patients' problems for which general practitioners seek help from a social worker? What do the doctors expect from their social worker? How do their patients present their problems to the social worker and what kind of help is she able to give them? What does a social work caseload in general practice look like? Is it true, for example, that some problems are spotted earlier in this setting than in a welfare agency and that it offers good opportunities for preventive work? What kind and what proportion of needs presented by patients should be met and dealt with by the general practice team itself and what kind of problems are easily transferable to other social agencies? How can social work in general practice be efficiently organised and how can general practice best relate to existing social services in the community and particularly to the reorganised personal social services?

After describing the background of the project, the area in which it was located, its methods of procedure, and the roles and relationships as they evolved among the team, we shall outline the main characteristics of the patients who were referred to the social worker. We shall then consider the kinds of problems these patients presented to their doctors and trace how the original complaint was translated into a referral for social work and finally into 'a social problem'. We shall go on to describe the processes of social work, both within the practice and in collaboration with many other agencies in the community. Finally, we shall draw tentative conclusions from this experience and ask some questions about its possible implications for the future organisation of the social services and medicine.

REFERENCES

ANDERSON, J. A. D., DRAPER, P. A., KINCAID, I. T. and AMBLER, M. C. (1970), 'Attachment of Community Nurses to General Practices: A Follow-up Study', *Brit. Med. J.*, *4*, (103–5).

BACKETT, E. M., MAYBIN, R. P. and DUDGEON, Y. (1957), 'Medicosocial Work in General Practice', *Lancet*, *i*, (37–40).

BRITISH MEDICAL ASSOCIATION, Planning Unit (1970), *Primary Medical Care*. London, BMA.

24   SOCIAL WORK IN GENERAL PRACTICE

COLLINS, J. (1965), *Social Casework in General Medical Practice*. London, Pitman.
COOPER, B. (1971), 'Social Work in General Practice: the Derby Scheme', *Lancet, i*, (539–42).
DEPARTMENT OF HEALTH AND SOCIAL SECURITY (1971). *Reorganisation of Group Practice*. London, HMSO.
DICKINSON, K. G. and HARPER, M. (1968). 'Aspects of Social Work in General Practice', *J. Roy. Coll. Gen. Practitioners, 15*, (96–106).
DONGRAY, M. (1958), 'Social Work in General Practice', *Brit. Med. J., 2*, (1220–23).
DONGRAY, M. (1962), 'Co-operation in General Practice: a Medical Social Worker Replies to a Doctor', *Almoner, 14*, no. 12, (547–56).
FORMAN, J. A. S. and FAIRBAIRN, E. M. (1968), *Social Casework in General Practice*. London, Oxford University Press.
HARWIN, B. G., COOPER, B., EASTWOOD, M. R. and GOLDBERG, D. P. (1970), 'Prospects for Social Work in General Practice', *Lancet, ii*, (559–61).
JEFFERYS, M. (1965), *An Anatomy of Social Welfare Services*. London, Michael Joseph.
MCCULLOCH, J. W. and BROWN, M. J. (1969), 'Social Work in General Medical Practice', *Med. Soc. Wk., 22*, (300–9).
MARTIN, M. (1970), 'Towards a Mental Health Social Work Service for General Practitioners, *Social Work, 27*, no. 4, (7–11).
PATTERSON, J. E. (1949), 'The Work of the Almoner in General Practice: an Alternative Approach, *Almoner, 1*, no. 11, (230–33).
RATOFF, L. and PEARSON, B. (1970), 'Social Casework in General Practice: an Alternative Approach', *Brit. Med. J., 4*, (475–7).
REPORT of the Committee on Local Authority and Allied Personal Social Services (1968) (Seebohm Report). Cmnd. 3703. London, HMSO.
ROYAL COLLEGE OF GENERAL PRACTITIONERS (1970), *Present State and Future Needs*. London, RCGP.
ROYAL Commission on Medical Education (1968), *Report*. Cmnd. 3569. London, HMSO
SCOTT, R. (1965), 'Medicine in Society', *J. Roy. Coll. Gen. Practitioners, 9*, (3–16).

2

THE AREA

The project was based in a practice a few hundred yards from the main shopping street of Kentish Town, a densely populated district in the London Borough of Camden. Well served by public transport, the practice catchment area extends north to the attractive districts of Hampstead and Highgate with the large expanses of Hampstead Heath, and south to St Pancras and Holborn, which has three terminal railway stations, many office-blocks and the University of London Senate House with its many ancillary buildings. The immediate neighbourhood of the practice was changing rapidly during the time of the project due to extensive demolition and housing developments. Many of the privately owned and multi-occupied Victorian houses were being purchased by the local authority and converted into self-contained flats. However, a considerable proportion of overcrowded, multi-occupied dwellings remained in the area. (Centre for Urban Studies 1968.)

In Camden in 1966 nearly half the households were still lacking in one of the basic amenities such as an inside lavatory, piped hot water or a bath (G.R.O. 1967). There was also an acute shortage of small dwellings for one- and two-person households. This affected many of the elderly patients of the practice who lived in large and inconvenient accommodation. On the other hand, many large families lived in overcrowded conditions, particularly those in furnished accommodation prevalent in Camden, which has the third highest proportion of furnished lettings in Greater London.

Camden, although it is in some respects typical of other Inner London boroughs, has special characteristics which affect social and medical care in the area. It contains the Senate House of London University and many colleges and 23,000, or 10 per cent of the Borough's resident population, are students. Two big teaching hospitals and many other specialist medical teaching units are concentrated in Camden. Of the Borough's population, 27 per cent were born outside Britain, the largest groups coming from Ireland and Europe (in contrast to the immigrants from 'new commonwealth' countries in other Inner London boroughs). Camden also has one of the highest mobility rates in Inner London—16 per cent of the population had moved into their home within the year preceding the 1961 census. The age-structure of the Borough reflects its mobility, since there are proportionately few children, but many people between the ages of 15 and 45 of whom a much higher proportion than in Greater London are single, widowed or divorced. Camden is well known as a bedsitter land—34 per cent were single households in 1966 and 46 per cent of households were in shared dwellings. Certain features of social pathology in Camden may be related to its peculiar social structure—for example, the comparatively high rate of suicides, deaths from cirrhosis of the liver, and possibly also the high illegitimate birth-rate (G.R.O. 1970).

The employment structure of the Borough is also relevant to understanding the practice population and its potential needs for social work. Of the employed Camden residents in 1966, 45 per cent were women (a higher proportion than in Greater London) and of these 41 per cent were married. Some 70 per cent of the Camden residents were engaged in service employment and approximately one-third were office workers. A fifth of the labour force worked in professional and scientific services, a much higher proportion than in Greater London, clearly reflecting the presence of so many seats of learning in the area.

Health and Social Services in Camden
A survey of general practice carried out in Camden in 1968 showed that, compared with other parts of the country, Camden's residents were also well supplied with general practitioners.[1] In certain respects, however, general practice in Camden differed from the country as a whole. Only one in seven of the general practitioners were in partnerships of three or more, and over half were single-handed, while in England and Wales half of all practitioners were in partnerships of three or more. Compared with the country as a whole, Camden general practitioners were badly housed and poorly equipped, they were less well provided with secretaries, receptionists, attached nurses and health visitors and a smaller proportion than in the country as a whole had appointment systems.

The group-practice on which the project was based belonged to the 12 per cent of the Borough's practices which had a nurse and/or a

[1] Jefferys, M. *Personal Communication.*

health visitor attached, or which employed secretarial staff. It belonged to the 15 per cent of Camden practices which did not take private patients. The partners allocated a special sum from fees received for certificates for example to a patients' fund which the social worker used a good deal.

Camden is richly provided with in-patient and out-patient general hospital facilities. The Borough contains two teaching hospitals whose patients come from a wide geographical area; these hospitals have well-staffed social work departments and each hospital has several other general hospitals in their 'group'. The big psychiatric hospital which catered for the catchment area of the general practice was six miles from the Borough and the large hospital for mentally subnormal patients was also outside the Borough.

The Borough health and social services were comparatively well staffed. In 1967 all except three of the forty-four health visitors in the Borough worked from infant welfare clinics and only two health visitors were attached to general practice. The local authority health department ran a special geriatric service which was staffed by twenty-three health visitors, the only local authority workers decentralised into small teams.

The local authority departments concerned with the social services (Children's, Health and Welfare) were housed together in a building which was a ten-minute bus ride or one tube stop from the practice. In 1967 some fifty-six social workers were employed in the Health and Welfare Departments and forty in the Children's Department. Many developments affecting the care of mentally ill and handicapped people were initiated in Camden at that time, but most did not come to fruition until the later months of the project. These included an industrial training centre, a junior training centre for handicapped children and two hostels, one for adults and the other for disturbed adolescents, all of which were due to be opened in 1968.

The local authority Health Department had a family service section consisting of a team of about ten social workers. Their functions were to provide casework help for families in difficulties, to co-ordinate the social service functions of other departments and to keep a register of families 'at risk'. The Welfare Department was staffed by twenty-seven social workers and seven trainees, and was concerned with the needs of homeless families, of physically disabled people and with some aspects of care for the elderly. In 1967 Camden employed 205 'Good Neighbours' who were local people, usually working part-time. The simple services they gave to the ill and disabled supplemented the work of home-helps. In 1967 the 205 Good Neighbours outnumbered the 193 home-helps also employed in Camden.

Thus the project was located in a comparatively rich London borough with its share of social problems and with above average medical and social facilities.

REFERENCES

CENTRE FOR URBAN STUDIES (1968), *Housing in Camden. Vol. 2. Report on the Housing Rents Study*. London, London Borough of Camden.

GENERAL REGISTER OFFICE (1967), *Sample Census 1966, England & Wales County Report. Greater London*. London, HMSO.

GENERAL REGISTER OFFICE (1970), *The Registrar General's Statistical Review of England & Wales for the Year 1968—Pt. 1, Tables, Medical*. London, HMSO.

JEFFERYS, M. (1971), *Personal Communication*.

3

THE PRACTICE TEAM

The practice is housed on a corner in a four-storey Victorian building; like others in the street it has a somewhat run-down appearance. Its large lofty rooms have been converted into three surgeries with adjoining examination rooms, the nurse's treatment room and three rooms for secretaries, the health visitor and the social worker. A sizeable kitchen on the top floor became a common room where the staff could eat, talk or rest. The waiting-room on the ground floor houses a toy-cupboard, budgerigars and a fish tank. The somewhat shabby, homely, non-clinical appearance of the building matches the warm and friendly atmosphere inside which is usually full of chatter, laughter and people, and has none of the hushed air sometimes associated with medical settings. Friendliness, spontaneity and informality are the keynotes of the relationships between members of the staff and between staff and patients. This lack of status-consciousness and the outgoing friendliness to allcomers makes an immediate impact on an outsider entering the practice, and has an invigorating and therapeutic effect.

At the start of the project in June 1965 the team consisted of four doctors with a list of some 9,000 patients, a part-time consultant on marital and sexual problems, a full-time secretary, a practice nurse, two receptionists and a full-time health visitor who had been seconded to the practice by the Camden Health Department since 1964. There were major staff changes at the time the social worker arrived; two partners who had been with the practice since its inception had left. These two doctors had been part of the earlier planning for the attachment of a social worker to their team; the two partners who succeeded them arrived a few weeks before the social worker. During the project another partner joined the practice and a second health visitor was appointed in 1968.

All members of staff participated in discussions about practice matters and there was an implicit assumption that good general practice included concern and help for social and emotional problems. In many ways the partners, the nurse and the receptionists had been engaged in welfare work on behalf of their patients long before the health visitor and the social worker arrived in the practice. There was little possessiveness about 'my patient' and the concept of the Caversham Centre was adopted deliberately. The patients had their own doctors, but were free to make an appointment to see another doctor; in time they seemed to develop an attachment to the Centre and transferred easily to other doctors in emergencies or holidays. In such a setting the introduction of a social worker into the team presented few difficulties. Patients were accustomed to being referred to others in the team and on the whole interpreted referral to the social worker as a sign of special concern.

Functions of the Team

In order to put the social work into context it is essential to understand the roles and functions of the practice team and to realise how such a setting differs from a social service department in a local authority with its administrative constraints, or a voluntary casework agency with its strong professional emphasis, or from the hierarchical setting of a hospital social work department.

The Caversham Centre often seemed full of people who were rushing in different directions; there was an atmosphere of tension and pressure, a feeling that all the staff were on a knife's edge of time, and a good deal of noise and laughter and apparent muddle. Everyone was too busy to be anything but himself—irritable, as well as spontaneously kind. Affection for patients was freely expressed—especially if they were in trouble. This contrasted strongly with the formality in hospitals, where staff may wear white coats or other 'badges' of office, and with local authority departments, where the greater size of a Town Hall organisation may mean that the reception area is separated from practice. In this situation waiting people do not have the opportunity to get to know the rest of the team by sight, or to observe them as ordinary people under pressure. It differs, too, from some voluntary casework agencies where emphasis on teaching can take a high proportion of the staff time needed for case discussion and supervision of younger staff and students.

Indeed, the Caversham Centre seemed to be much more community-based and orientated towards its neighbourhood than many local authority departments which, until the recent reorganisation into area teams, often served large districts. All the practice staff, except the health visitor and social worker, lived in the vicinity, hence some patients were their friends and neighbours.

The Secretary
In describing the members of the team, it is perhaps unusual to start with the secretary. However, she was in certain respects the centre of the practice and held all the strings in some sort of order. She was single-handed in the early years of the project, being responsible for the doctors' correspondence, accounts, banking, executive council returns, the wages of all the staff, for arranging surgery rotas, duty calls and locums, and for calling ambulances. She also saw to the day-to-day administrative problems of the building. It was the secretary who put new toilet-rolls in the lavatory, saw that there were electric light-bulbs, rang the plumber, bought the food for the doctors' lunch-time meetings and provided cleaning materials. When later on she acquired an assistant she was able to devote her considerable administrative abilities to other essential tasks, such as helping to compile an age-and-sex register. The social worker used the secretary as a kind of barometer of tension and always consulted her about any new plan which would make demands on the time and energy of the practice staff. The secretary's assessments usually turned out to be correct and her discplined approach—she often described herself as 'the practice nagger'—ensured that enthusiastically made plans were carried through to some sort of conclusion. Although somewhat fearful that the project would impose additional strain upon the practice, the secretary became one of its most enthusiastic supporters. She also became convinced of the importance of collecting basic data about patients and the on-going work of the practice.

The Practice Nurse
It was impossible to be in the practice for more than a few days without becoming aware of the affection with which the nurse was regarded by many patients. She was known to everyone by her first name, prefixed by 'Nurse', and her's was the truly open door to people in need. Many patients who went directly to her room with minor complaints were seeking comfort and reassurance for their anxieties as much as treatment for their pains and bruises. She often became closely involved with people who were elderly or chronically ill. Over a number of years, she had for example, given care to a refugee who was schizophrenic. This patient slept in a derelict house and often came just to sit and have a cup of tea. The people who came to see her

may have had a quarrel with their husband or a row with an adolescent child; an elderly person may have experienced a sudden flood of loneliness after a bereavement. They knew that they did not have to produce a physical symptom in order to sit in her room, nor did they have to talk about any problems if they did not wish to. It often occurred to us that such a room in which a sympathetic person was consistently available, without demanding anything in return in the way of 'activity', would be an ideal addition to any day-care facilities for the chronically mentally ill or for those who are depressed and tired.

The practice nurse's attitude towards the social work project was positive from the start, and her referrals to the social worker showed sensitive and intuitive recognition of stress. On occasions she would discuss patients and her relationship with them, without necessarily referring them to the social worker. She was surprised to find that the social worker 'approved' of her involvement with patients. From the beginning, the nurse and the social worker talked the same language; there was no competition between them and they collaborated closely on many occasions. For instance, the social worker would ask the nurse to reassure patients who might be nervous about coming to the practice for examinations or tests.

The Health Visitor
The health visitor and the social worker did not achieve collaboration so easily. The question most often asked at the start of the project was 'Will the health visitor and the social worker get along well?'—the implication being that they might not work happily together. Thus, within and from outside the practice, a lot of inhibiting attention was directed towards their relationship.

The health visitor had been working in the practice for eighteen months by the time the social worker arrived and her work had made a considerable impact. She had a caseload of 500 families and had extended and developed the antenatal and well-baby clinics which already existed. This work had revealed a volume of need which had not been anticipated by the practice and which was out of proportion to the size of the premises and the time of the staff. A crowd of mothers and their under-five children came to the baby clinic; waiting mothers and children spilled out into the only spare space—a landing above a steep flight of stairs on which toddlers played. The social worker arrived in the middle of this time of pressure, when the practice team had begun to realise that preventive health-care meant reorganisation of their timetable and priorities. The doctors realised that an extra member of the team, far from 'saving the doctor's time', can create work by doing it well.

The doctors knew little about the training or the work-methods of a social worker. Hence they could not visualise clearly how her role might complement that of a health visitor, who hitherto had dealt with the social problems arising in young families. The doctors were not helped by the inability of the social worker and health visitor to define their roles clearly. In the event, an arbitrary decision was made; all families with children under five, as well as families with children of school-age who had been known to her, sometimes fleetingly, in the past should be referred automatically to the health visitor. This division of function according to the criterion of the client's age, rather than by type of problem or the skill required in tackling it, implied that the health visitor and social worker did the same sort of work; it ignored differences in training, experience and methods of work and assumed that because both workers were concerned with social and emotional aspects of patient-care, their roles were inter-changeable. Nobody liked this arrangement, but everybody tried to make it work in the hope that a more flexible system would evolve. Inevitably it caused tensions between the health visitor and the social worker, despite their personal goodwill and friendliness towards one another. For example, a doctor might refer a patient with a marital difficulty to the social worker without paying attention to the fact that there was a young child in the family. This could arouse suspicion in the health visitor and, in turn, lead the social worker to refuse such a case although she could have been of help.

Eventually the health visitor and the social worker realised that this enervating situation was depriving patients of the most appropriate service. Fortunately, they shared concern for the patient, a sense of humour and common sense. They decided that they could not resolve the traditional anxieties of their two professions which were both in a state of change; they could only work out a better differentiation of function in their own situations. Collaboration gradually increased during the second year and some misconceptions were corrected. For example, the health visitor had expected that the social worker would do all the social work for patients in the practice by herself; she had not realised that the social worker would view part of her job as mobilising other resources in the community and introducing outside workers to the practice team. Together the health visitor and the social worker organised conferences on difficult cases at the practice

c

and invited workers from other fields, thereby sharpening their awareness that these families required help from other people in the community as well as from the practice team. In this way the roles of both
the health visitor and social worker could be seen in perspective
against broader horizons.

In the course of their work the health visitor and the social worker
learned much from each other. The health visitor's contact with
younger families who were usually healthy and functioning well
impressed on the social worker the importance of the health visitor's
preventive role in detecting early signs of family and social breakdown
and underlined how essential it was for the health visitor as well as
the social worker to be knowledgeable about other resources in the
community. The teaching content of a health visitor's work was
also more fully appreciated by the social worker, who remembers
being present when a mother and her new baby who had been born
with a hare-lip and cleft palate, came to see the health visitor. The
mother was crying from exhaustion and the baby screaming with
hunger because the mother did not know how to help him feed. In an
hour the health visitor had taught this mother to feed her baby. The
health visitor began to see how the social worker's skills could be
used with families who experienced social and emotional difficulties
that did not respond to normal educational or advisory methods. Both
workers also recognised the area of overlap between them and saw
that particular circumstances of individual families may over-ride
otherwise valid divisions of function. For example, the health visitor
herself may want to deal with complex problems in families she had
come to know well, perhaps consulting the social worker about
specific aspects of their difficulties. In some families there may be a
role for both health visitor and social worker, and yet in others the
social worker may take over the health visitor's routine supervisory
function for a time, while working with a young couple on their
marital problems.

During the last year of the project the health visitor left to take up
a teaching appointment where she is encouraging joint teaching
sessions for health visitor and social work students. While overcoming
their professional problems, the health visitor and social worker
developed a conviction about the value of interprofessional education,
and since leaving the practice their friendship has continued. The two
succeeding health visitors had lighter caseloads; both were especially
interested in social casework, and they and the social worker discussed their cases freely. At the end of the project they were

considering possibilities of combining to help patients by group discussions.

The Receptionist

Another central person whose activities and observations impinged greatly on the social worker was the receptionist. She had been with the practice for six years, knew many patients well and was another person to whom they often talked about their problems. To house-bound patients who telephoned for repeat prescriptions, she was their personal link with the practice. They called her by her first name and, although they seldom saw her, regarded her with affection since she usually found time for a chat. The receptionist had exceptional social skills, especially with disturbed children. In the morning several children, whose mothers went out to work, would come in to spend the odd half-hour with her until it was time for school. She made skillful referrals of children who were not going to school or who spent too much time at the surgery, or who demanded what she considered undue emotional support. In the waiting-room she sensed which people were in pain or especially anxious or depressed. She knew which patients wished to wait quietly in a corner, and how much noise she could allow from children without upsetting others. The receptionist was also the guardian of records and the frustrated manager of an appointment system which, like many others, did not always work very well.

The junior receptionist had worked at the practice since leaving school. Her referrals were usually communicated to the social worker through other people, as she would discuss them first, with the doctors, the senior receptionist or the secretary, whose assistant she later became.

The Doctors

The doctors, of course, formed the core of the general practice team. Their approach to social work differed in important respects, according to their professional experience and personalities. The senior partner had built up this group practice since 1952 and had done much of the pioneering which led to the appointment of health visitors and social worker. He maintained the momentum of the project in the early months, referring for the first two years twice as many patients to the social worker as did the other partners. He was particularly interested in the rehabilitation of unemployed patients and in the difficulties of young people. His long-standing knowledge of, and interest in, social work enabled him to select for referral patients who could make good use of social work.

The second partner had been with the practice for many years and was skilled in obstetrics. He often had close relationships with his patients who sometimes found it difficult to form a therapeutic relationship with anyone else. Because he had many babies on his list he had a close working relationship with the health visitor, and he looked to the social worker for help with some of his patients who were chronically ill.

The third and fourth partners had joined the practice only very shortly before the appointment of the social worker. The third, previously a hospital physician, had to come to terms with the lack of hierarchy in the practice. His first referrals seemed designed to test the skills of the social worker, as though he was asking, tongue in cheek,

'Does she expect to cure chronic, multi-problem situations?'

Beneath his jocular manner he had concern and interest for emotional problems. Before referring a patient he would obtain and write a comprehensive social history, and follow this with half an hour's discussion with the social worker. This careful assessment and preparation often enabled the patient and the social worker to come to grips with the problems straight away.

The fourth partner had worked for many years in an industrial community in Scotland. She had wide experience of poverty and disease in a hard-working, closely-knit community; she was especially interested in the needs of old people and skilled in predicting difficulties and in evolving ways of intervening before a crisis. From her came a suggestion that the social worker should keep a register of vulnerable elderly patients; these frail people often lived alone and were only just managing to cope. This register was started in the first year of the project and the names of all vulnerable elderly people known to the practice team were given to the social worker. This doctor naturally expected social work to provide services and meet material needs. The first case she referred was an elderly woman who needed a home-help as she had broken her arm. This patient was not sure that she really wanted any domestic help, as this made her feel old and dependent; To her this accident foreshadowed her impending old age and helplessness. The social worker not only induced her to accept the home-help, but also discussed her fears about the future. To the social worker's surprise the doctor showed little interest in the emotional problems aroused by the patient's accident but was solely concerned with the arrangement of the home-help. This in turn made the social worker realise that her medical colleagues were often too busy to be especially interested in all the emotional repercussions, but had to focus on what they saw as the main problem. For many months this doctor referred people for 'a little chat', but found it difficult to understand why a social history could not be obtained in ten minutes and why social workers needed any training beyond a comprehensive knowledge of available services. It is perhaps a small indication of the success of the project that this doctor is now one of the most lucid exponents of the functions and skills required by social workers and of the way in which they complement those of the medical practitioner. She described the differences between a patient's interview with a general practitioner and a social worker thus:

'In a surgery interview the general practitioner leads the way to a diagnosis by pinpointing questions. A social worker follows the patient to an assessment by listening to his anxieties and asking clarifying questions only at salient points.'

The Social Worker
The project social worker who joined this team had a generic social work training and had worked previously in a family casework agency. She had worked in London for some ten years and, like any experienced social worker, had a reasonably wide knowledge of the available statutory and voluntary resources. Like the health visitor, who had formerly worked for an infant-welfare clinic, she had no experience of functioning within such a close-knit, multi-disciplinary team who shared a small building and whose relationships differed from the more hierarchical structures found in hospital or clinical teams. The social worker had been accustomed to some formality in her relationships with senior colleagues, most of whom were women. Members of the practice team greeted new members with informal friendliness and expected the social worker to follow their practice of using Christian names.

The social worker was fortunate in obtaining a part-time secretary who had done temporary secretarial work in the practice for some years. In time her work extended far beyond secretarial duties, for she learned to compile and code the statistical information for the study and took responsibility for arranging domiciliary services and searching for suitable social clubs or holiday homes. Sometimes she interviewed clients in connection with these arrangements. In effect, she worked as an assistant to the social worker and accomplished these varied tasks in her sixteen hours a week.

Establishing Communications

An understanding of how members of the team worked and what they expected from the social worker developed gradually in a variety of ways. To begin with, the unwritten rules in the practice, as in any other team, had to be identified and respected if frayed tempers were to be avoided. Removing the medical notes from the receptionist's files without telling her where they were, interrupting the secretary when she was taking dictation, or the nurse when she had patients awaiting her or the health visitor on baby clinic afternoons, were obvious intraventions of rules. There were also rules for avoiding more delicate points of stress. The doctors shared the surgeries and they, the receptionists and the nurse had no rest-room of their own and so came to the kitchen to drink coffee or read the paper. Sometimes they used the kitchen as a meeting-place to discuss practice matters. At other times they needed just to sit and speak to nobody for a while, especially if they were weary after a busy surgery. It could be hard to resist the temptation to discuss a pressing problem with somebody who was apparently sitting and doing nothing. The team evolved one rule for the benefit of the social worker: not to interrupt her if she was speaking with a patient. One rule the social worker asked of the practice was that the only copy of her record on a patient should not be removed from her file and sent to a clinic to which the patient was being referred.

As sixteen patients were referred to the social worker during her first ten days at the practice, she did not have spare time for long, but the interaction during these few leisurely days was important. One afternoon the social worker sat in the waiting-room to experience its atmosphere, and during her first week each doctor took her on a special 'home visiting' round. The social worker was apprehensive lest patients should mind this intrusion, but quickly realised that housebound people appreciated their doctor's efforts to keep them informed of developments in the practice. Usually he would say

'We have a social worker in the practice now—I thought you would like to meet her.'

Often she stayed to chat with these patients and their families and sometimes discovered that they were not receiving services which could help them, or that they were receiving regular assistance without their general practitioner being aware of it. The social worker was surprised at this lack of communication and from 'being introduced' as the newcomer, she quickly started to introduce local social workers to the practice team—often they had worked in the same locality with the same patients for years without a personal meeting.

In order to make the project realistic and to get as close an estimate as possible of the prevalence of psycho-social problems in the practice, the social worker and the doctors decided that she should accept all referrals, however busy she was. After all, general practitioners cannot close their doors or start a waiting-list. The doctors undertook not to refer patients whose transient difficulties could be solved by time or those whose long-standing problems had either been fully explored by other social agencies or were unlikely to respond to social work help. It was also agreed from the beginning that as much use as possible should be made of the social agencies in the community and that only those patients who seemed to need help in the practice setting should receive this from the social worker herself.

Initially the doctors' way of referring patients to the social worker was by a note, scribbled on a scrap of paper during consultation and clipped to the medical notes.[1] These referral notes were brief, colloquial and vivid, and very different from the long accounts social workers tend to write to each other when referring cases. Used to writing lengthy reports of her interviews with patients, the social worker found that she had no time for these in general practice, nor was it necessary for the team to know about her interviews in such detail. Initially the team wished to see if she knew her job, but not how she did it. The need for brief records and a more appropriate type of feedback was obvious.

A weekly staff-meeting was already held at lunchtime in a small surgery. Its purpose seemed mixed; to discuss clinical and social problems and to make administrative arrangements. The room was packed with people, either standing or sharing chairs, and there was continual movement in and out with little real discussion taking place. Often when the health visitor was trying to focus attention on one of her urgent problems, the discussion would rise to a crescendo with several people trying to talk at the same time. There was no chairman or agenda. Informal discussions happened continuously, over tea and coffee, or gathered round the nurse's or receptionist's desk until the group was moved on by the person trying to do her work. People

[1] Examples of referral notes are given in Appendix A.

drifted into the social worker's room, possibly to sit in the armchair and feel a little protected from the constant demands in the rest of the building. The social worker spent much time in the first weeks listening and discussing in a relaxed way anything the partners or members of the team brought up. The doctors asserted they knew little about the social and psychological background of their patients, but it soon became apparent that they had stored up a great deal of knowledge which previously they had had no occasion to put into words.

Although informal discussions enabled the social worker and other members of the practice team to get to know one another and to learn something about their 'set' towards their work, this was not enough. There was a clear need for regular and more orderly case discussions between all members of the practice in order to develop a common language, common concepts, and a clearer understanding of the different skills involved in helping patients. Twice-weekly case discussions devoted to social problems were arranged over lunch in the kitchen, attended by the entire practice team. On another day the doctors and the practice secretary had a lunchtime meeting at which they discussed practice and clinical matters. Thus, three hours each week were put aside for discussion. Attendance was optional, but there were seldom absentees. In these meetings the members of the team slowly revealed to each other their different approaches to problems, their different expectations of what was possible, and also their common aims. The social worker soon learned that the type of case discussion appropriate to a general practice differed from that in a social work agency where an hour may be spent considering one family.

In the beginning it was assumed by the practice that between fifteen to twenty cases would be discussed in an hour, consisting of brief questions like What is the problem? Can we help? If not, who can? The content and nature of these meetings changed rapidly. Soon by general consent the number of cases discussed was reduced to between five to ten in each meeting. At first only the health visitor and social worker brought up cases and no one was in charge of the meetings. The absence of a chairman meant that discussions did not always result in a clear decision about action or responsibility. The lack of an agenda meant that time was wasted while someone refreshed his memory from the medical notes. Eventually it was decided that members of the team would act as chairman in turn, an agenda of cases would be compiled beforehand, and the medical notes put on the table during the morning. The secretaries volunteered to record decisions and file these in the medical notes.

As links were established with other helping people, the number of visitors to these meetings increased, until during one month visitors appeared at every meeting. This was too much and the team said so. It became clear that the working team needed time together in private, and outsiders were limited to alternate meetings. Sometimes at the beginning of these closed meetings, there was chat and a clear reluctance to get down to the agenda. When new to the practice the social worker found this bewildering and sometimes irritating, but quickly realised how important this respite was to herself and her colleagues. After working hard all the morning the refreshment of informally meeting together and having time for each other was sometimes an essential prerequisite to concentration on the problems of patients.

There were few difficulties over the use of medical or social work jargon, as all members of the team preferred simple words, but there was unsuspected confusion over the use of everyday terms; for instance, over the use of the word 'chronic'. When the social worker asked the doctors to reverse their original decision not to refer 'chronic' situations to her, it was discovered that the doctors attached the label 'chronic' to social problems which had never been clearly identified or referred for social work. The assessment of 'chronic' could be based on the duration of the difficulty, the weight and size of the medical notes, or the number of demands the patient had made upon the practice. When such difficulties were examined more closely the seemingly chronic situations sometimes began to look more like unmet need over a long period. Another common phrase was 'a psychiatric case'. This could refer to a patient who had seen one or many psychiatrists, a patient who had gross personality problems, or one of very low intelligence. Another term which was probably imported from social work jargon was 'intensive work'. This could mean that there were psychological difficulties which needed tackling in depth, or that a great deal of time had to be spent to resolve a crisis, or that something approaching long term psychotherapy was needed.

There were also interesting differences in approach and perception. For example, the time-perspective of doctors and social workers can differ greatly. A doctor sometimes thinks that crises arising in intractable, long-standing situations ought to be resolved quickly. Because he has to make quick decisions he may find it difficult to accept that people take time to decide, for example, whether to apply to enter an old people's home. To the doctor the issue is clear-cut, that the person is not managing in his own home, is in physical danger from oil stoves or gas cookers and seems depressed and lonely. Both the social worker and the doctors modified their attitudes towards time; the social worker's understanding that the patient hesitates and needs to go through a period of indecision did not preclude quick action on occasions, and the doctors developed more tolerance towards indecision.

Different approaches to 'judgemental attitudes' were noticed. Social workers sometimes assume that they do not make value-judgements. Most social workers now recognise that they, like other human beings, are embedded in their cultural and moral prejudices, although their training may enable them to gain insight into the direction of these prejudices and to acquire some measure of control over them. Doctors may feel angry with a family which does not care adequately for an elderly relative who is ill and not able to manage on his own. The doctor may urge that 'the family should be made to take responsibility'. The social worker learned that an authoritative approach could be helpful; it was possible to initiate frank discussion about such a situation with the family, even using such old fashioned concepts as 'duty' and 'obligations', sorting out what the old person needed and what the family were able and willing to do. Judgemental attitudes of 'right' and 'wrong' were also encountered in the sphere of marital conflicts. Some members of the team were inclined to feel that men were always in the right and others were equally sure that the women were being victimised. Usually, somebody was 'at fault'. A member of the team remarked one day: 'Nobody can help with marriages, can they?' The doctors were interested to learn that methods were being developed for understanding marital conflict in terms of mutual projections of frustrated needs and that it was sometimes possible to bring about resolutions of these hidden problems. The doctors became interested, for instance, in the work of the Institute for Marital Studies at the Tavistock Centre. Gradually, a good many marital problems were referred to the social worker and also to other agencies outside the practice.

The lunchtime meetings reinforced the mutual support members of the team could give each other in the face of uncertainty and of problems about which they could do very little. The social worker began to realise the full force of the expectations that patients put on their doctors to be certain, or at least reasonably sure, about diagnosis and treatment. Similarly the doctors often looked to the social worker to produce a diagnosis of family problems when she felt very uncertain about what was wrong. It was a great relief when eventually everyone could admit to uncertainty and lack of knowledge in many situations. The inclusion of receptionists, nurse and secretary in the case discussions ensured that their observations were taken into account, and this pooling of knowledge and experience from many vantage points often led to a new understanding of familiar or 'chronic' problems. Team discussions proved a great help in facing seemingly hopeless situations. Intractable problems yielded to objective analysis, positive and negative factors emerged more clearly and realistic plans could be evolved. These discussions also made it clear that a social worker was apt to unravel the complexities of human problems and so to cause more work rather than less, at least in the short run. Occasionally the doctors remarked that knowing about their patients' difficulties and family problems made life more complicated. Yet they continued to give much time to the discussion of social problems.

4

SOCIAL WORK ROLES

Changes in Social Work Method
At the beginning the social worker shared the assumption of many caseworkers that change was likely to be accomplished by long-term contact and regular, lengthy interviews, and that if clients came for only two or three interviews this could be regarded as a failure. The challenge of teamwork in general practice and the questioning attitudes amongst colleagues at the National Institute led to changes in the social worker's approach. For example, the time-pressures and the need to keep an open door led to experimenting with intensive episodic short-term work. In such cases a lot of help was given at the point of crisis and contact loosened as the patient or the family gave signs of being able to manage alone. Again, the necessity to refer many patients to outside agencies led the social worker to re-examine the type of relationship she formed with her patients, for if this relationship was too intense and dependent, transfer would be more difficult, and if it was too superficial, the patients might feel that the social worker had not understood their problems and was in a hurry to push them on to somebody else. It was not always easy to obtain the right balance and, at the same time, to reassure the patient that he was always free to return to any member of the general practice team.

The social worker began to revise her ideas about appointment systems. On the one hand she wanted to fulfil her obligations to patients who were receiving regular help from her, on the other, she wanted to remain accessible in emergencies and for consultation with doctors and other members of the team. The social worker gave up trying to interpret every failed appointment as 'resistance' and learned to cope flexibly with the reality of life in general practice. She found that ten minutes could be squeezed out of most days in order to see patients whose needs were immediate and who had no appointment. Although she came from an agency where one hour's session was the rule, she was able to experiment with lengths and types of interviews. She also found herself working at far greater speed than she had ever done before. While previously she had generally waited for people to lead her to the questions they wanted her to ask and was much more passive, she was now more positive about asking questions. She began to realise that if somebody brings up a subject it usually means he wants to be asked about it. She felt that her former approach had often left the patient to struggle alone and to do the work, as it were, unaided. Encouraged by the more unselfconscious and natural way in which the doctors proceeded, she found herself freer to ask questions, to express her own opinion, to give advice, to be more spontaneous and to grasp the nettle with her patients. We have no means of knowing for sure whether these changes were for the better. The social worker realised that she had never been so unreliable in keeping people waiting for appointments or changing times, but on the other hand, she had never felt so close to clients. The social worker also changed her ideas about working hours and often worked in the evenings. Some people had a long journey to work, others were doubtful about the value of social work and not very highly motivated to go through with it. They may have been too depressed or have recently recovered from an illness. Some had just been able to re-establish themselves in work, and it would have been unrealistic to ask them to take time off.

Another way in which the general practice setting differed from a social work agency was the absence of follow-up. In general, the social worker and the doctors felt that it was the patients' right to choose whether they kept an appointment and not to be sent follow-up letters, especially as they had opportunities of discussing matters with their doctors if they wished. Patients who improved might no longer attend the surgery while those who continued to feel unwell or anxious might continue to come. Like the rest of the team, the social worker met many patients informally in the vicinity. Some clearly felt better and said so. Continued contact with people who had made only limited progress or with those whose situation was deteriorating provided renewed opportunities to alleviate the situation. An important aspect of work in a general practice setting is that if a first attempt to help does not succeed, the patient will usually provide the practice team with further opportunities.

The Social Worker's Teaching Role
Teaching was an intrinsic part of the role of the practice for, like others, it accepted students from medical, health visiting and nursing courses. These students came for different lengths of time, ranging from a single visit of two hours to three months' full-time participation. A trainee

general practitioner was a member of the practice team for a year after qualifying as a doctor. To the social worker, collaboration with these recently qualified doctors was one of the most rewarding experiences of her work, for they invariably had a keen interest in the social and psychological problems of their patients and wanted to learn how they themselves could give help. They sought information about the social services and guidance about how to use them; having a light workload and keen concern, they were enthusiasts for taking action. Their criticisms and questions were challenging; often they would highlight gaps in the services.

Medical students who spent a few weeks in the practice expected to visit patients with the social worker, as they did with the doctors. After selecting and consulting patients, the social worker took these students with her and was often surprised that moderately severe material problems, like overcrowded or dilapidated accommodation, greatly shocked these young people. She learned not to take them into conditions which would severely distress and depress them, unless they were likely to be in the practice long enough to show them some of the encouraging aspects of community life too, like a well-functioning day centre. It was also important that time for adequate discussion with the student was available. Chronic and progressive physical or mental illness met in the community often impinged on them with a greater force than similar conditions seen during a teaching round in hospital. Accompanying social problems like loneliness, family conflict and shortage of money had often not been realised. In general practice, consideration of these factors was obviously an inescapable part of medicine.

One social work student came full-time for three months to the practice. This young social worker quickly gained the confidence of the practice team and learned much from them and from sharing her opinions with students from other disciplines who were also in the practice. The doctors invited her to sit in during their surgeries, and the nurse and health visitor also enabled her to observe them at work. The social worker became aware of some of the differences in the student/teacher relationship and in the methods of fieldwork instruction that exist in medicine, health visiting and social work. Unlike the medical students, the social work student was given her own caseload and interviewed her patients alone. She was also expected to give deliberate attention to her personal prejudices and attitudes as they impinged upon the problems of her clients. She was alerted to the types of relationship clients made with her and how these relationships influenced her ability to help them. In the training of doctors and health visitors the implications of a therapeutic relationship were usually picked up by observing the supervisor at work, rather than by systematic discussions which are customary in the field-training of social workers.

A community service volunteer came to work at the practice for a year between leaving school and training as a nurse. The health visitor used her services often; she gave much needed help with the baby clinics and toddlers' clinics. One very successful venture, suggested by the health visitor, was the help she gave to the Indian wife of a man who had to maintain a strict diet when a gastric ulcer was diagnosed. This woman spoke little English and did not understand European food. The volunteer visited her twice each week for several months. On the first visit she prepared and cooked the meal while the wife watched and wrote down in her own language what was happening. On the second visit the wife cooked and the volunteer watched. The peak moment of every visit was when they all sat down together to eat. The eventual successful integration of this young volunteer into the practice resulted in another volunteer succeeding her.

Methods of recording
It soon became apparent that the usual social work recording methods, consisting of narrative accounts of varying completeness, would not yield comparative data on all the clients the social worker was seeing. After about a year's exploration, during which we discovered which items of information should be recorded about everyone, we designed a simple record card.[1] Practically all the information on this card was precoded so that the fifty items of information required took only a few minutes to fill in. We recorded the referrer's name, the date of referral, the patient's age, civil state, occupation and living group; type of housing, source of income if unemployed or retired, the problems a patient presented to his doctor, what help the doctor requested from the social worker and what problems the patient finally presented on his first visit to the social worker. We noted whether any other agencies were involved now, or in the past, and what action the social worker intended to take after the first interview. The record card also contained a check-list of the problems as they were revealed during the course of the contact, the number of office interviews and home-visits, which members of the household were in contact with the social worker and for how long, and what social

[1] A copy is reproduced in Appendix B.

agencies were contacted on behalf of the patient. Finally, we indicated what action was taken, reasons for closing the case and the outcome in the social worker's and the patient's opinion. The data were then transferred to coding sheets and punched onto cards. The distribution of the various items of information and their percentages were analysed by computer which was also used for relating items of information to each other.

The difficulties encountered in recording and analysing information relating to on-going social work were much greater than anticipated. To give a picture of patients and their problems at one point in time is comparatively simple, but to devise an information system indicating changes is a different story. For instance, the same patient may have been referred several times during the four years of fieldwork; his civil state may alter, his problems may change and so will the kind of help he may be offered. Thus 'episodes' had to be distinguished from 'people'. Some information was meaningful only in terms of people— for example, age, sex, social class; other information relating to the kinds of problems presented and action taken needed to be analysed in terms of episodes. These problems of appropriate data collection and analysis are, of course, not peculiar to social work. Most hospitals and treatment statistics, for example, refer to attendances or admissions, yet record linkage requires information which refers to people, showing changes over time. After much trial and error we achieved a workable system of analysis, but we did not solve the complex problems inherent in analysing the on-going processes of social work among a changing client population. Although the social worker found the discipline of standardised recording irksome at times, as the project went on, she became an enthusiastic supporter of statistics as a way of monitoring social work. The recording system could not have been kept up as efficiently without the social worker's part-time secretary who made sure that the index cards were completed and who transferred the information to coding sheets. An interim analysis of the data at mid-point of the project produced the first dividend of the recording system. We learned many surprising facts about the social worker's caseload and the action she had taken (Goldberg *et al.* 1968). Although the social worker intended to add narrative accounts of interviews to her record cards, the pressure of work and the size of caseload made it impossible to describe the interactions between social worker, client and other agencies in the detail in which she would have wished. Often she also would have preferred to take the patient's living group or his family as the basic client unit, rather than the registered patient, since her work was not infrequently centred on those who were well and carrying the burdens in the family.

Another notable gap in the analysis of the data was the lack of information on medical diagnosis in relation to referrals for social work, to social problems emerging and to type of action taken. Thus questions about which kinds of conditions throw up what kinds of social problems could not be explored. A serious attempt was made to record the medical diagnosis of patients referred to the social worker during one year, but the formidable difficulties inherent in this exercise defeated us. First of all, the general practitioners found it difficult to attach a diagnosis to the many ill-defined signs and symptoms of which patients complained; secondly, the time factor proved a difficulty—a past illness (for instance, a mental breakdown or a coronary attack) may be as relevant to the need for social work as the present pathology; thirdly, multiple pathology which was often characteristic of the patients in need of social work could not always be squeezed into a 'primary' and 'secondary' diagnosis. We also noted that the doctors were inclined to code 'psycho-neurosis' as a primary condition, even in cases where the symptom was subsidiary to a serious physical illness, because it was a psychological difficulty which occasioned the referral to the social worker. It is hoped that future projects will be able to devote more time and resources to studying the relationship between medical diagnosis and social problems than we were able to do.

REFERENCES

GOLDBERG, E. M., NEILL, J., SPEAK, B. M. and FAULKNER, H. C. (1970), 'Social Work in General Practice', *Lancet, ii,* (552–5).

D

PART II

THE CASELOAD

5

THE SOCIAL WORKER'S CLIENTS

We want to describe first the main characteristics of the patients who were referred to the social worker and to explore whether they differed from the practice patients and the general run of people residing in the neighbourhood.

How Many?

1,009 people were referred to the social worker during her four years at the practice. Of these patients 179 were referred a second time, 52, three times and 19, four or five times (Table 5.1). Thus the social worker dealt with 1,352 'episodes'[1] during these forty-eight months, an average of 28 a month or 6 to 7 referrals per week.

Table 5.1

NUMBER OF PEOPLE REFERRED TO SOCIAL WORKER
JULY 1965–JUNE 1969

Number of times referred	Number of people	Number of episodes
1	759	759
2	179	358
3	52	156
4	16	64
5	3	15
Totals	1,009	1,352

NOTE: Totals do not necessarily agree from table to table due to varying numbers of people for whom information is complete. Where appropriate, percentages have been rounded to nearest whole number and adjusted so that they add to 100.

[1] An episode consisted of a referral which resulted in either no personal contact or one or more interviews at the office or elsewhere, extending over any length of time. If no contact between patient and social worker had occurred for twelve consecutive weeks, the episode was considered closed. A new episode started if further contact took place subsequently.

During the first three months of the project 168 patients were referred, twice as many as in most of the succeeding quarters (Table 5.2).

Table 5.2
NUMBER OF REFERRALS IN THREE-MONTHLY PERIODS

Year	Quarter	Number of referrals
1965	July–Sept.	168
	Oct.–Dec.	108
1966	Jan.–Mar.	65
	Apr.–June	97
	July–Sept.	80
	Oct.–Dec.	64
1967	Jan.–Mar.	95
	Apr.–June	72
	July–Sept.	66
	Oct.–Dec.	87
1968	Jan.–Mar.	86
	Apr.–June	81
	July–Sept.	63
	Oct.–Dec.	59
1969	Jan.–Mar.	86
	Apr.–June	75
	All referrals	1,352

Clearly the doctors had been earmarking situations which they wished to bring to the notice of the social worker when she arrived. After the first six months the flow of cases settled to a fairly steady average of 25 a month or 5 per week. The small differences in the three-monthly figures can be partly explained by the social worker's holidays, study-leaves of doctors, and twice (in March 1966 and in July 1967) referrals were stopped for one month to allow the social worker to get up to date with recording. It is also our impression that there was an un-spoken awareness by the practice of the maximum number of cases the social worker could comfortably accept and deal with. It is worth noting too that the Consultative Committee expressed concern about the large number of cases which had been referred during the first six months. The 1,352 episodes which came to the notice of the social worker certainly did not represent all the social problems which were brought to the practice during these four years. Many other patients with psycho-social difficulties were either helped by the doctors themselves or by other members of the practice team, and undoubtedly some problems went unrecognised.

About a quarter (239 people) of those referred did not have an interview with the social worker; the reasons for this are shown in Table 5.3.

Table 5.3

REASONS FOR NOT BEING INTERVIEWED BY SOCIAL WORKER

Reason for no interview	Number of people
Direct referral to other agencies	92
Other social workers active	48
Telephone contact only	21
Refused referral	9
Did not keep first appointment	36
Not suitable for social work	5
Died or moved away	4
Different reasons on different episodes	23
Not known	1
Total	239

The largest group, 92 of those not seen, simply required an introduction to other helping agencies in the community. For example, an 84-year-old widow, living alone, depended upon her neighbour in the same house for meals, domestic help and company. Their house was being emptied for conversion and the neighbour was rehoused at short notice. The neighbour then wrote to the general practitioner explaining that the old lady now alone in the empty house would not be able to manage. Clearly, immediate provision of meals-on-wheels and a home-help was required, as well as contact with the geriatric visitors and speedy co-ordination with the housing department. Another example is that of a 23-year-old privately-employed nurse from Malaya who became seriously ill and had to be admitted to hospital. She had no family in the United Kingdom. The experience of losing her job and becoming a patient frightened her. She was referred directly to the medical social worker in the hospital who was on the spot and so was able to help her more effectively than the social worker in the practice.

Among patients referred but not seen, 48 were already in touch with other social workers. The most effective way of helping them was by establishing communication between the general practitioner and the social worker concerned. This was often achieved by arranging a case conference at the practice between all concerned. Another group of 21 people were passing through a transitory crisis which could be resolved by a telephone contact. For example, a 58-year-old widow, in close touch with her general practitioner, had her supplementary benefit cut for no apparent reason. Telephone conversations with the patient and the local office of the Department of Health and Social Security led to a restoration of her benefit. At the same time information about her eligibility for allowances for extra needs was passed on to her doctor.

Forty-five patients were not interviewed because they refused to see the social worker. Only 9 patients refused explicitly in discussion with the doctor, but 36 refused implicitly by not keeping their first appointment. Discussion with the doctors about this group indicated that these patients had possibly more social and psychological problems than patients who accepted referral. This tends to confirm findings from other studies (Morris 1964) that the non-co-operators are often those with the severest pathology and may be in the greatest need of help. In five instances the social worker considered the problem was not suitable for her intervention. Thirty-two patients were not seen for a variety of other reasons including situations where help was given to the patient's relatives rather than directly to the patient.

Age and Sex
The age distribution of the social work patients was markedly different from that of the practice patients and of the Camden population (Table 5.4).

Whereas 22 per cent of the practice population and 15 per cent of the Camden population were under 15, only 2 per cent of the social work patients were under 15. This may be a slight underestimate as in some instances the parents consulted the doctor about their own distress rather than presenting the child as the person in need of help. The division of work between the health visitor and social worker meant that many families with children were automatically referred to the health visitor. The other striking feature is the excess of elderly people referred to the social worker—28 per cent were over the age of 65 compared with 10 per cent in the practice and 13 per cent in Camden. This discrepancy is even more pronounced for those over the age of 75 where the social worker dealt with four times as many as one would expect from their representation in the practice. As will be seen from Table 5.4 the proportion of young adults and the middle-aged patients

Table 5.4

AGE AND SEX OF SOCIAL WORK CLIENTS, CAVERSHAM PRACTICE PATIENTS AND CAMDEN POPULATION

(Percentage distributions with ratio of men to women in each age group in brackets)

Age	Caversham social work clients*			Caversham practice patients†			Camden population‡		
	Men %	Women %	Total %	Men %	Women %	Total %	Men %	Women %	Total %
0–14	3 (42)	2 (58)	2	24 (52)	20 (48)	22	17 (51)	14 (49)	15
15–19	7 (31)	7 (69)	7	6 (49)	5 (41)	5	7 (45)	7 (55)	7
20–24	10 (31)	10 (69)	10	8 (41)	10 (59)	9	10 (44)	11 (56)	11
25–44	28 (30)	29 (70)	29	34 (48)	32 (52)	33	30 (51)	26 (49)	27
45–59	17 (29)	19 (71)	18	17 (48)	17 (52)	17	21 (47)	21 (53)	21
60–64	8 (41)	5 (59)	6	4 (46)	4 (54)	4	6 (46)	6 (54)	6
65–74	12 (35)	10 (65)	11	5 (41)	6 (59)	6	6 (38)	9 (62)	8
75+	15 (27)	18 (73)	17	2 (27)	6 (73)	4	3 (30)	6 (70)	5
Total %	100 (31)	100 (69)	100	100 (47)	100 (53)	100	100 (47)	100 (53)	100
Number	310	689	999	4,244	4,808	9,052	101,610	115,480	217,090

* Age at first interview † Derived from 1967 Practice List ‡ General Register Office (1967)

in the social worker's caseload resembled the proportions prevailing in the practice and in the area. In short: hardly any children of school age or younger were referred to the social worker, but a third of her patients were over the age of 60. The age-structure of patients referred to the social worker attached to a general group practice in two other recent social work projects in general practice (Forman and Fairbairn 1968, Collins 1965) were similar. Of the social work patients in the Barnstaple practice 28 per cent were over 65 and of the Cardiff patients referred to the social worker 33 per cent were over 60.

At the Caversham centre, among those patients referred to the social worker but not interviewed there were even fewer young people and considerably more elderly patients than among those who were referred and received an interview. Nearly half (48 per cent) were over 60 and 34 per cent, a third, over 75. Many of these elderly patients were referred during the early months of the project by the doctor who was concerned about frail elderly people who might be in need of domiciliary services in the near future. A special register of vulnerable elderly patients was compiled and eventually most of these people were referred for supervision to the local authority geriatric visitors whose functions were described in the previous chapter.

Over twice as many women as men were referred to the social worker, 689 compared with 310. This is in striking contrast to the sex ratio in both the practice and the Camden population where women exceeded men by only 6 per cent. Comparing the sex ratios of the social work patients with the practice population and the Borough population in the different age-groups we find that the greatest deficiency of men occurs in the age-band 25–59 (Table 5.4). Of the social work clients in this age-group 30 per cent were men in contrast to the practice and the population of Camden where approximately 50 per cent were men. In the preretirement period between the ages 60 and 65 the sex ratio is very close to that of the practice and the Camden population and it also approximates the norm in the age-groups above retirement. Again, very similar sex ratios were found among the social work patients in the other two experiments, namely 28 per cent males in Barnstaple and 34 per cent in Cardiff.

One can speculate on the reasons for the differences in these sex distributions. Although the practice population was almost evenly divided between men and women, a study of surgery attendance revealed that women attended one-and-a-half times as often as men during the five years 1965 to 1970. We found the greatest disparity in the middle years, where women consulted their doctors twice as often as men, while among those over 60, women and men had similar attendance rates. Thus one important reason for the marked preponderance of women in the social worker's caseload, particularly in the middle years, could be that their greater frequency of attendance at the practice put them more 'at risk' of being referred. However, the nature of the problems probably also contributed to the different sex ratios; disturbances in marital and family relations predominated, as will be seen in later chapters. Women may thus be performing their traditional 'expressive' roles as the family spokesman for social and emotional problems. Such difficulties are also often associated with anxiety, minor depression and personality disturbances. Higher rates in women for neurosis and psycho-social problems have been reported in general practice in London (Shepherd *et al.* 1966). As we have seen, men make proportionately fewer appearances in their general practitioner's surgery at the peak period of their working lives, but disabilities of late middle age combined with cumulative anxieties about retirement bring them to their doctor in their late fifties and sixties; the repercussions of these anxieties may come within the scope of social work.

Marital Status
The widowed (22 per cent), the single (30 per cent) and the divorced and separated (10 per cent) constituted 62 per cent of all the social work clients compared with 49 per cent in the Camden population.

In every age-group a larger proportion of social work clients were widowed, divorced or separated than in the Camden population, although census figures do not distinguish people who are separated. Information emerging on the marital status of clients in a national sample of cases carried by social workers in local authority health and welfare departments show similar trends.[1] Such findings tend to confirm Townsend's findings in relation to the elderly (Townsend and Wedderburn 1965) that it is those with little or no family support who are most in need of social help. It is worth remembering that the health visitor dealt with many young families who, with a different division of labour, might have found their way to the social worker.

Household Composition
The preponderance of the elderly, widowed and divorced is clearly related to the large proportion of one-person households among the

[1] I.e.'Workloads of social workers in Local Authority Health and Welfare Departments' (work in progress at the National Institute for Social Work Training).

Table 5.5

MARITAL STATE BY AGE OF SOCIAL WORK CLIENTS COMPARED WITH CAMDEN POPULATION

(Percentage distributions)

Age	Caversham social work clients					Camden population*			
	Number in age-group (= 100%)	Single	Married	Widowed	Separated/ Divorced	Number in age-group (= 100%)	Single	Married	Widowed/ Divorced†
15–24	170	82	14	0	4	38,100	85	15	—
25–44	284	24	58	2	16	60,510	35	62	3
45–64	234	18	47	20	15	58,430	20	68	12
65–74	105	14	31	49	6	16,670	20	50	30
75+	163	17	17	65	1	10,000	18	30	52
All those over 15	956	30	38	22	10	183,810	39	51	10

* General Register Office (1967).   † Published census figures do not distinguish 'Separated' from 'Married' nor 'Widowed' from 'Divorced'.

client population—35 per cent compared with 14 per cent in Camden (Table 5.6).

Over half of the social work patients aged 60 and over lived alone and over a third of young people in their twenties lived by themselves. At the other extreme, 25 per cent of the social work clients lived in large

Table 5.6

SIZE OF HOUSEHOLD OF SOCIAL WORK CLIENTS COMPARED WITH CAMDEN POPULATION

Number of persons in household	Households* of Caversham social work clients		Camden population	
	No.	%	No.	%
1	349	35	28,230	14
2	236	24	50,220	26
3	164	16	39,330	20
4	117	12	35,040	18
5	68	7	20,550	11
6 or more	56	6	22,280	11
Total	990	100	195,650	100

*Where different clients come from the same household, the household is counted only once.

households containing four or more people compared with 40 per cent in Camden. Indeed, only 26 per cent of the households, just over a quarter, contained children of school age and under (Table 5.7).

This again may be related to the health visitor's role in the Caversham practice, as she was more likely than the social worker to be in touch with families containing children and particularly large families, who are more prone to problems related to developmental difficulties (Rutter *et al.* 1970). A small proportion of the households consisted of married couples living without children (Table 5.7). Thus the social worker's caseload was predominantly composed of people living alone or in small two-generation families. In only a few instances did members of the extended family or non-related people form part of the household.

Social Class

We have seen that the age and sex distribution of the patients referred to the social worker differed significantly from the practice population

Table 5.7

HOUSEHOLD COMPOSITION OF SOCIAL WORK CLIENTS
(Percentage distributions)

Composition of household	Number of clients
Client living alone	35
Married couple only	13
One adult* with children under 15	3
Married couple with children under 15	11
Other households with 2 or more adults* } with children under 15	12
Other households with 2 or more adults*	26
Total %	100
Number	990

* Adult—a person aged 15 or over.

and the residents of Camden. The social work patients' marital state and household composition were likewise not at all representative of the Borough. Surprisingly their social-class distribution was similar to that of Camden (Table 5.8).

In order to arrive at an exact comparison with the census data for Camden we are presenting the figures for men only. Table 5.8 shows some under-representation of professional people among the Caversham social work clients which may possibly be related to the fact that the practice catchment area did not include the most affluent parts of Hampstead and Highgate. We note an over-representation of unskilled workers among the Caversham clients which may be associated with the practice's location in the heart of Camden's working-class area. However, if—in view of the very small numbers involved—we combine the first two groups (professionals, employers and managers) and the last two groupings (semi-skilled and unskilled workers) then the differences between the Caversham social work clients and the Camden population are negligible. An examination of the women's social class as determined by that of their husband or, where appropriate, by their own occupation, suggested that the social-class distribution of the whole client group was very close to that of Camden.

This match in social class between the social work clients and the neighbourhood may indicate that when a social worker functions in

Table 5.8

SOCIO-ECONOMIC GROUPINGS OF CAVERSHAM CLIENTS
COMPARED WITH CAMDEN POPULATION

Socio-economic groups	Caversham* social work clients No.	%	Camden population† No.	%
3 & 4 Professional (including self-employed)	11	5	6,200	8
1, 2, 13 Employers, managers	24	11	9,000	12
8, 9, 12, 14 Other self-employed and skilled	63	30	21,240	29
5 & 6 Non-manual	63	30	19,470	27
7, 10, 15 Service, semi-skilled, agricultural	19	9	11,000	15
11 Unskilled	31	15	6,770	9
Total	211	100	73,680	100

* Includes only economically active and retired males, and excludes groups 16 and 17, i.e·
the Armed Forces and inadequately described occupations.
† General Register Office (1967).

a setting which brings her into contact with a cross-section of the population a similar proportion in all social groups are found to need her help. This suggestion finds confirmation in the Barnstaple project where the social class composition of the social work patients was also very similar to that of the local population. However, the nature of the problems may differ from one social class to another as we shall show later on.

Housing
Comparing the housing situation of the social work clients with that of Camden (Table 5.9) we see certain differences.

Somewhat fewer of the patients referred to the social worker owned their homes and considerably more lived in local authority property. Here again it is worth remembering that the practice did not include the most affluent districts; also at the time of the social worker's attachment an intensive local authority rebuilding programme was at its height in the immediate vicinity of the practice.

The number of amenities such as the exclusive use of a fixed bath

Table 5.9

HOUSEHOLD TENURE OF CAVERSHAM CLIENTS
COMPARED WITH CAMDEN POPULATION
(Percentage distributions)

Household tenure	Caversham social work clients	Camden population
Owner occupied	12	17
Rented from L.A.	47	25
Rented privately:		
Furnished	18	17
Unfurnished	23	41
Total %	100	100
Number	853	186,910

was slightly greater among the social work patients than for the whole of the Camden area, possibly because a higher proportion of the patients lived in recently converted or newly built local authority property.

At least 100 (10 per cent) of the social worker's patients lived in accommodation which she considered to be clearly unsuitable for them. This judgement was based upon the patient's health needs, as, for example, when disabled people were housebound because of stairs they could not negotiate or when elderly people had difficulties with inconveniently situated lavatories. Sometimes housing conditions exacerbated the patient's illness, as in the case of a bronchitic old man living in a damp basement.

A quarter of the patients referred to the social worker had either recently moved or were expecting to move. This was clearly connected with the Borough's building programme, but also with the mobility of young professional people and students. These actual and potential changes created some anxiety, particularly among the older patients.

Summary
About a thousand patients were referred to the social worker in four years and there were twice as many women as men. Over a third of them were elderly and two-thirds were either single, widowed, divorced or separated. Thirty-five per cent lived alone and the rest mainly in small households. Their occupational distribution was similar to that of the Borough—that is to say there was no weighting towards the lower social classes. Of the social work patients, 10 per cent were

found to live in housing conditions which were inimical to their health, but in general their housing was reasonably satisfactory and reflected the active housing programme of the Borough.

REFERENCES

COLLINS, J. (1965), *Social Casework in General Medical Practice*. London, Pitman.

FORMAN, J. A. S. and FAIRBAIRN, E. M. (1968), *Social Casework in General Practice*. London, Oxford University Press.

GENERAL REGISTER OFFICE (1966), *Census 1961. England and Wales. Greater London Tables*. London, HMSO.

GENERAL REGISTER OFFICE (1967), *Sample Census 1966. England and Wales County Report. Greater London*. London, HMSO.

RUTTER, M., TIZARD, J. and WHITMORE, K. (1970), *Education, Health and Behaviour*. London, Longman.

SHEPHERD, M., COOPER, B., BROWN, A. C., KALTON, G. W. (1966), *Psychiatric Illness in General Practice*. London, Oxford University Press.

TOWNSEND, P. and WEDDERBURN, D. (1965), *The Aged in the Welfare State*. London, Bell.

MORRIS, J. N. (1964), *The Uses of Epidemiology*. Edinburgh. E. & S. Livingstone.

E

6

THE PATIENTS' PROBLEMS AND THEIR PATH
TO THE SOCIAL WORKER

How did the patients come to the notice of the social worker? In the majority of cases the process of referral started with a consultation between patient and doctor. It is instructive to trace the various stages in the patient's journey to the social worker and to see how the original complaint was translated into a referral for social work and finally into a 'social problem'. The questions we are going to ask are 'What were the patients' complaints to the doctor in the first place?' 'What requests did he make to the social worker on their behalf?' 'How did the patients present their difficulties when they first met the social worker?' and finally, 'How did these difficulties relate to the problems that eventually became the major concern between the patient and the social worker?'

Throughout the following discussions we shall refer to patient 'episodes', since 25 per cent of the patients were referred more than once during the four years, often with different complaints arising in changed social situations.

Just over three-quarters of the referrals (77 per cent) came from the doctors, 5 per cent from other members of the practice, 13 per cent from patients themselves (mostly second episodes occurring in the later stages of the project) and a small number (5 per cent) from outside agencies.

A great variety of situations were referred to the social worker by the practice team, scribbled down on a prescription pad[1], or in face-to-face discussions and, later, on specially designed forms. In order to carry out any kind of comparative analysis we had to think of some means of classifying these diverse problems which emerged from the interaction between doctor and patient. After a year's verbatim recording of the phrases used in the referrals we decided on a crude and simple system of classification based on what had brought the patient to the doctor on this specific occasion and had given rise to

[1] See Appendix A for examples of referral notes.

the discovery or suspicion of a social problem suitable for referral to the social worker: was it a physical illness that had occasioned the referral, for example, bronchitis or a vague symptom for which no immediate cause could be ascertained, such as an inability to sleep, headaches, lack of concentration? Was it a psychiatric illness, or was it a frank social problem without any complaint of illness, for example, a marital or parental difficulty? These four broad categories—definite physical complaints, vague psychosomatic symptoms, psychiatric illness and overt social problems covered all of the situations which led the doctors to ask for help.

Table 6.1

PROBLEMS PRESENTED BY PATIENTS TO DOCTORS

(Percentage distributions)

Problems presented to doctors	*Interviewed by social worker*	*Not interviewed by social worker*	*All* episodes*
Definite physical complaints	37	56	42
Vague psychosomatic symptoms	34	15	29
Psychiatric illness	11	13	12
Overt social problems only	18	16	17
Total %	100	100	100
Number†	775	267	1,042

* These figures represent only those episodes which were referred by the doctors.
† Totals may not always agree from table to table due to varying numbers of people for whom information is complete. Where appropriate, percentages have been rounded to nearest whole number and adjusted so that they add to 100.

About 42 per cent of the problems presented by the patients in their contact with the doctors related to definite physical symptoms, either experienced in themselves, or in another member of their household (Table 6.1), ranging from terminal illness to a passing attack of influenza. Progressive illness in which patients inevitably deteriorate and terminal illness can bring many social needs and stresses in their train; social problems also frequently arose with patients who were chronically ill or permanently disabled and among those who suffered prolonged bouts of illness at certain times, notably men with bronchitis. Acutely ill patients who had experienced or were dreading major surgery were referred with many emotional and social problems. Other patients found themselves in a sudden social crisis occasioned by debilitating infectious illness. In such circumstances a minor illness may give rise to gross anxiety or inability to cope.

About a third of the patients referred to the social worker complained of vague psychosomatic symptoms to the doctors who detected or suspected underlying social or psychological problems.

A small proportion (12 per cent) of those thought to be in need of social work were mentally ill and in these cases the doctors were particularly concerned with the many social repercussions of mental illness affecting these patients, their families and the immediate community in which they lived. There were financial difficulties, problems of finding suitable jobs; occasionally more dramatic situations were encountered, such as the destitution of the young drug addict, the bankruptcy of a gambler, the social deterioration of an alcoholic, or the desolation of the patient who had attempted suicide.

Nearly a fifth of the patients came to the doctor complaining only or mainly of a distinct social problem. These were related not only to obvious difficulties in family relationships but also to worries about work, housing or to emotional problems such as anxiety and loneliness.

It will be noted from Table 6.1 that the patients who did not actually see the social worker more often presented a physical complaint than those who were seen (56 per cent compared with 37 per cent). As we saw in the last chapter, a high proportion of these patients were elderly. They were often frail and incapacitated and in need of specific domiciliary services and of somebody who could keep an eye on them. Such patients were referred directly to the appropriate agency, for example, the geriatric visitors employed by the local authority Health Department. On the other hand, far fewer of the patients not interviewed by the social worker complained of vague symptoms. One explanation is that by their very nature most of these complaints demanded personal investigation by the social worker in the first place, rather than a referral to another agency.

The Doctors' Requests to the Social Worker

The next link in the chain of the referral process is the request made by the doctor to the social worker. These requests were expressed in many different explicit and implicit messages, and once more we decided, after a period of observation and sifting, on comparatively broad headings.

Table 6.2 shows that among the patients who saw the social worker

Table 6.2

REQUESTS MADE BY DOCTOR TO SOCIAL WORKER

(Percentage distributions)

Requests	Interviewed by social worker	Not interviewed by social worker	All episodes*
Social assessment	41	22	36
Provision of services	33	63	41
Casework	26	15	23
Total %	100	100	100
Number	775	263	1,038

* These figures represent only those episodes which were referred by the doctors.

the doctors asked for three kinds of help in differing proportions. They asked for a social assessment in 41 per cent of the episodes, for provision of services in 33 per cent and for casework in 26 per cent of the episodes.

In contrast, the doctors asked for the provision of services in nearly two-thirds (63 per cent) of the cases not interviewed (Table 6.2). As we have already seen, they included more elderly people who were passed on to the geriatric visitors for preventive care, and others whose only need was to be linked with other social services.

When we now turn to examine what the doctors asked the social worker to do and relate these requests to the complaints which brought the patient into the surgery, we find interesting differences (Table 6.3).

Table 6.3

PROBLEMS PRESENTED BY PATIENT TO DOCTOR

AND REQUESTS MADE BY DOCTOR TO SOCIAL WORKER

Problems presented by patients to doctor	Requests made by doctor to social worker			
	Social assessment	Provision of services	Casework	All* episodes
Definite physical complaints	50	285	100	435
Vague psychosomatic symptoms	218	31	55	304
Psychiatric illness	45	51	21	117
Overt social problems only	62	54	66	182
Totals	375	421	242	1,038

* These figures represent only those episodes which were referred by the doctors, whether or not the patient was in fact seen by the social worker.

In over half the episodes related to physical illness the doctor asked the social worker for the provision of services. This was more than a simple request for meals-on-wheels or a home-help, which would be dealt with by the practice secretary. A request for the provision of services to the social worker could imply that suitable resources were not readily available or that patients and their relatives needed special help to accept and use services that were ready at hand. Such patients sometimes felt at odds with the authorities who provided this help, either because they misunderstood the functions of the services or were reticent about approaching 'welfare' agencies. In such cases the doctor was really asking the social worker to interpret the patient's individual needs and to secure more flexibility which might enable a particular patient to make use of the help available. Sometimes no appropriate service existed to meet the patient's requirements. Physically and mentally disabled people often have needs for simple services which are difficult to find; for example, someone who will sit with an elderly or dying patient in his home, or someone who will take a patient out for a walk in a wheelchair, or look after the pets of a patient going into hospital or on holiday. In such situations voluntary effort and goodwill in the local community had to be sought. Sometimes the request for provision of services meant that the services supporting a patient were not working in unison or in tune with the patient's feelings. A common example is the loss and grief experienced by elderly and vulnerable people when their home-help is transferred without warning or explanation. One old lady had many sleepless nights worrying whether her home-help had met with an accident before she gathered the courage to ask her doctor to inquire on her behalf. Another example of the need for co-ordination is the effort required for rehousing the very old. A very frail couple aged 87 and 89 were pleased to be offered a new flat in a protected housing scheme, but dreaded the move itself. This couple knew what they wanted done and needed help from people who were calm, efficient and able to co-ordinate many last-minute arrangements. For example, the carpet and curtains needed cleaning before they moved, but these old people could not climb, kneel, lift, carry or walk far, and volunteer help was enlisted to deal with the lino and curtains. Gas and Electricity Board workers arrived promptly in response to a special request and this couple moved without becoming flustered or ill.

In over 70 per cent of the episodes presenting a vague psychosomatic complaint the doctors asked the social worker for a social assessment, sensing that she might uncover social or psychological stresses in the patients' background. Most of these patients needed hardly any explanation or special encouragement to unburden themselves to the social worker. Inability to sleep, vague feelings of depression and tiredness or lethargy may mask long-standing worries which seem insoluble to the patient but which he had never discussed with anybody. Such symptoms may be a concealed cry for help from people who usually cope well with life but who are subject to extreme prolonged pressures and strains. For instance, such stresses could be felt by relatives of chronically ill patients. A vague physical and psychological malaise may be experienced by 'captive wives' in a restricted environment surrounded by small children and housework. In yet another context anxieties and conflicts about impending or actual retirement may lurk behind sudden frequent attendances with ill-defined aches and pains.

The social problems surrounding psychiatric illness mainly called forth requests for provision of services and for social assessment (Table 6.3). Services were often needed to meet the basic requirements of chronically mentally ill patients and those recently discharged from hospital—for instance, lodgings, assistance in finding a suitable job, help in establishing social contacts. A social assessment was requested frequently when patients had virtually exahusted all known treatment resources and the doctors would ask despairingly 'Is there anything else we could try?' Referrals for casework (in a sixth of the psychiatric cases) often implied that the patient's family was in need of support.

Finally, we come to the patients who complained to the doctor about an obvious social problem; in these cases requests for all three types of social work help were made in almost equal proportions (Table 6.3).

Problems Presented to the Social Worker at First Interview
What did the patients bring up as their trouble when seeing the social worker for the first time? In most cases the patients or their relatives saw the social worker by appointment for about an hour. This gave them ample time to unburden themselves. Many talked not only about what troubled them most acutely at that particular time—often a complex mixture of personal problems and external vicissitudes—but they would also delve into the past and describe the background to their problems. Thus a great deal of material emerged while the social worker was listening, asking clarifying questions. In comparatively simple situations she might offer suggestions and advice straight

away. However, in most cases the first interview was tentative and exploratory, social worker and patient trying to understand what the matter was and how to set about finding a solution.

When patients found themselves in an acute crisis, the helping process started at the same time; the very fact that someone was prepared to listen in a relaxed manner could bring relief, and occasionally what seemed hopelessly complex could be unravelled and appear manageable after all. More will be said later about the social worker's ways of helping. Here we only wish to point out that these first interviews were by no means as 'tidy' as subsequent tables might suggest. Many patients found themselves in a 'sea of troubles', and we realise that picking out one problem that seemed to preoccupy them most is artificial and does not do justice to the real situation. Nevertheless it seemed worthwhile in order to disentangle the process of referral and treatment to identify the main concerns expressed in the patient's first contact with the social worker; to relate these to the complaints previously presented to the doctor and also to the problems subsequently revealed.

Nearly a third of the patients expressed concern about family difficulties of various kinds in their first interview with the social worker (Table 6.4); nearly a quarter voiced anxieties about their health or found themselves in a personal crisis. A fifth of the patients were struggling with problems associated with mental illness or personality difficulties, 12 per cent were concerned about environmental problems such as housing and financial need and 9 per cent with difficulties at work or school.

Comparing the kind of problem brought to the social worker with the complaint presented to the doctor we find that over 40 per cent of the patients who discussed difficulties in family relationships in their first contact with the social worker had complained of vague psychosomatic symptoms to the doctor (Table 6.4). For example, a young married man in a semi-skilled job complained about inability to sleep and began to discuss his growing frustration with his marriage and family responsibilities—his attempt to train for more skilled work in evening classes had aroused resentment in his young wife who was tied to home and children. Of those who revealed family difficulties to the social worker, 30 per cent had presented their social problem straightaway to the doctor and 20 per cent had complained about definite physical symptoms. Financial need, housing problems and needs for domiciliary services were predominantly related to physical illness (Table 6.4) which was often chronic or progressive.

Table 6.4

PROBLEMS PRESENTED BY PATIENT TO SOCIAL WORKER AND PROBLEMS PRESENTED BY PATIENT TO DOCTOR

Problems presented by patient to social worker	Problems presented by patient to doctor				
	Definite physical complaints	Vague psychosomatic symptoms	Psychiatric illness	Overt social problems only	All* episodes
Problems in family relationships	49	111	17	76	253
Problems at work, school	20	32	7	10	69
Financial need, housing problems, need for domiciliary services	53	20	6	14	93
Anxieties about health, personal crisis	111	48	5	20	184
Psychiatric illness, personality difficulties, problems in social relationships	27	53	40	12	132
Others/Not known	25	2	8	9	44
Totals	285	266	83	141	775

* These figures represent episodes referred by the doctors in which the social worker saw the patients.

The majority of those who expressed anxiety about their health or more generalised anxiety to the social worker had presented physical symptoms to the doctor. Worries about the social implications of disabling symptoms were often expressed. For instance, a woman with an arthritic shoulder worried how she would be able to do her hair and dress herself as time went on. The impression was gained that some patients felt freer to air these anxieties to a lay person rather than to 'waste the doctor's time' which they thought should be given to people who were 'really ill'. While some patients thought that their fears were too trivial to tell the doctors, others felt that they were too serious to voice to someone who was qualified to give them the verdict they dreaded. For example, a middle-aged woman who had had abdominal surgery for a condition she feared was malignant wished to talk about her anxieties, before seeking a definite diagnosis.

Initial Problems Presented and Main Problems Revealed
So far we have described the way in which patients presented their problems to the doctor and the social worker when they first met them. Although most patients talked at length at their first interview, in about 40 per cent of the episodes their main difficulties did not emerge clearly until later in the contact, since for some patients, talking at length about themselves and their immediate environment was a novel and puzzling experience. Before entrusting the social worker with the problems that really bothered them they might want to understand her role in the team and to assess her as a helping person. The social worker, while listening, was busy weighing up the stresses in the patients' life situations, and trying to identify those which most impeded their social functioning. At the same time she would also consider which of the personal problems and environmental difficulties revealed seemed most susceptible to change, having regard to the resources available for help.

The main problems which thus emerged were not necessarily the most severe of the patient's difficulties—these were at times intractable and inalterable, given the relatively limited treatment resources available. For example, with a deserted mother who had severe personality problems, the main difficulties selected and tackled in the social work treatment were her relationships with her two teenage children which contributed much to her present unhappiness but were capable of some change.

Another point that needs consideration is that most patients had several inter-related problems. For example, an old man aged 86 suffering from chronic bronchitis suddenly lost his wife. He became badly undernourished as he could not cook and refused all domiciliary services. The indifference of his only married daughter and the damp and cold conditions of his basement flat contributed substantially to his misery and depression. In short, the personal crisis of bereavement seemed to exacerbate long-standing health and housing problems and defects in family relationships, all of which played a part in this man's problems.

Unfortunately we could not find a method of categorising the permutations of problems into a reasonable number of configurations or main types. We therefore reluctantly selected the main problem-area identified and tackled in each episode. This enabled us to relate the main problem to the characteristics of the patients and to the form of help they were receiving. We noted other problems present as 'subsidiary'. For instance, in the case of the old man just cited we recorded the crisis of bereavement as his main problem and parent/child relationships, housing and need for domiciliary services as subsidiary problems. This 'judgement' is not meant to indicate cause and effect. In many social and psychological conditions we are as yet ignorant about aetiology. The crisis of bereavement had to be tackled first and foremost, although the housing and family problems were contributing substantially to the crisis, and action was also initiated on them.

Examining the main problems revealed in the 1,020 episodes with which the social worker had personal contact over the four years, we find that a third were related to difficulties in family relationships of which almost half were marital troubles (Table 6.5). In about a fifth of the episodes practical needs were identified as the main problem: for money, housing or domiciliary services. In a similar proportion of episodes personal crises of various kinds and anxiety about health emerged as main problems. In 17 per cent of the episodes the main problem-area was related to personality and psychiatric difficulties and in 10 per cent to school and work problems.

If we compare the distribution of problems categorised as 'main' and 'subsidiary', as we have done in Table 6.5, we find that they are very similar. For example, difficulties in family relationships formed 30 per cent of the main and 30 per cent of the subsidiary problems. The only discrepancy occurs in the sphere of health and personal crises which were identified more often as main (19 per cent) than as subsidiary problems (10 per cent). This seems understandable in a general practice setting in which the social worker is readily available

Table 6.5

MAIN AND SUBSIDIARY PROBLEMS

Problem type	Occasions when problem type occurred as main problem No.	%	Occasions when problem type occurred as a subsidiary problem No.	%	Occasions when problem type occurred either as main or subsidiary problem No.	%
Problems in family relationships	282	30	574	30	856	30
Problem at work, school	92	10	215	11	307	11
Financial need, housing problems, need for domiciliary services	175	18	372	20	547	19
Anxiety about health, personal crisis	180	19	198	10	378	13
Psychiatric illness, personality difficulties, problems in social relationship	167	17	436	23	603	21
Others/Not known	57	6	105	6	162	6
Totals	953	100	1,900	100	2,853	100

in emergencies and crises. In general, these strikingly similar distributions of main and subsidiary problems may indicate that the social
worker did not consistently judge some sorts of problems as minor
and others as major; for instance, she did not relegate most material
and environmental problems to the subsidiary category, thereby
attaching more importance to emotional and relationship problems.

Since we worked on the assumption that people often do not reveal
their 'real' problems straightaway we want to examine whether this
assumption was justified in general practice. In Table 6.6 we compare
the problems initially presented to the social worker with the main
problems revealed, which shows that about 60 per cent of the patients
discussed their 'main' problems at the first interview.

For instance, three-quarters of those whose main problems emerged
as difficulties associated with family relationships indicated these difficulties from the outset. The unambiguous and early presentation of
family problems of many different kinds could reflect the practice
team's concern for the families of patients. Another possible explanation is that the social worker had previously functioned as a family
caseworker and was used to perceiving and exploring problems in
the context of family relationships.

In nearly two-thirds of the episodes in which the main problems
were associated with personal crises or anxieties about illness and
disability, patients discussed these with the social worker in the first
interview. About a fifth of the episodes with such problems presented
a family difficulty to begin with. For example, a recently bereaved
wife in her fifties who had dislodged her elderly mother from her flat
in East London asked for help in the future care of her mother, who
she said was totally dependent on her. It soon became evident that
this woman was deeply affected by the causes of her husband's death
and that her mother was a cheerful, independent, slightly confused
old lady, who was longing to get back to her own flat and her bud-
gerigar.

Difficulties at school or work emerged clearly in the first interview
in the majority (65 per cent) of the episodes.

On the other hand, patients experiencing difficulties in social
relationships because of deep-rooted personality disturbances or
chronic mental illness or patients who were socially isolated did not
reveal their difficulties so readily. Table 6.6 shows that 30 per cent of
these patients either concentrated on practical needs to begin with, or
expressed anxiety about their health and general situation. Another
group in which barely a half brought out their main problems at the

Table 6.6

INITIAL PROBLEMS PRESENTED TO SOCIAL WORKER AND MAIN PROBLEMS EMERGING

Initial problems presented to social worker	Main Problems Emerging						
	Problems in family relationships	Problems at work, school	Financial need, housing problems, need for domiciliary services	Anxiety about health, personal crisis	Psychiatric illness, personality difficulties, problems in social relationships	Others/Not known	All episodes
Problems in family relationships	245	12	16	37	13	12	335
Problem at work, school	6	65	4	2	18	3	98
Financial need, housing problems, need for domiciliary services	7	3	93	11	27	8	149
Anxiety about health, personal crisis	23	9	41	117	28	13	231
Psychiatric illness, personality difficulties, problems in social relationships	15	9	19	14	80	14	151
Others/Not known	7	1	14	5	9	20	56
Totals	303	99	187	186	175	70	1,020

first interview were patients who had practical needs. Not infrequently these patients accepted their circumstances as inevitable, unaware of the services that existed to help them.

Subsidiary Problems

As already mentioned most patients referred to the social worker had several inter-related problems. Only in 9 per cent of the episodes was there a single problem area, which was usually associated with straightforward material needs, for example, finding someone to look after an old lady's pets while she went on a recuperative holiday.

As Table 6.7 indicates, nearly half (45 per cent) of the patients had two subsidiary problems, about 20 per cent had one subsidiary problem only and nearly a quarter had three or more subsidiary problems.

People experiencing difficulties in social relationships, either on account of personality difficulties, psychiatric illness or because the environment was a stressful one had proportionately most subsidiary problems (34 per cent had three or more). The explanation is probably that mental illness and emotional difficulties are often associated with stresses in the family, at work and with general interpersonal difficulties. Patients whose main problems were related to family relationships also had many interacting subsidiary difficulties (Table 6.7). Difficulties in parent/child relationships and in the wider family group and personality disturbances were the most frequently occurring subsidiary problems in marital disharmony. This accords well with clinical experience. Marital strife often creates insecurity in children; personality difficulties in one or both partners can perpetuate a pathological pattern of interaction; and in-law troubles can accentuate and deepen divisions.

A crisis can arise in many different contexts. Thus a personal crisis was associated with family problems, difficulties at work, financial need, housing and community relationships in almost equal proportions. For example, a crisis occasioned by sudden illness can be aggravated because key relatives are unable to help at the right time; a bereavement can be more devastating if the husband who has taken a good deal of time off to nurse his wife loses his job as well. Illegitimate pregnancy can bring homelessness, financial need and social isolation in its train.

Relationship of Problems to Illness

In a general practice one would expect most of the social problems

Table 6.7

MAIN PROBLEM EMERGING AND NUMBER OF SUBSIDIARY PROBLEMS*

Main problems emerging	No. of subsidiary problems					Total	Average no. of subsidiary problems*
	0	1	2	3	4 or more		
Problems in family relationships	19	45	127	39	47	277	2.2
Problems at work, school	4	23	48	11	1	91	1.4
Financial need, housing problems, need for domiciliary services	24	46	72	16	15	173	1.7
Anxieties about health, personal crisis	18	48	77	18	18	179	1.8
Psychiatric illness, personality difficulties, problems in social relationships	8	24	76	32	24	164	2.2
Others/Not known	14	12	21	6	4	57	1.5
Totals	87	198	421	122	133	941	

* This table excludes early episodes for which subsidiary problems were not recorded.

† Where there are four or more subsidiary problems, we have calculated these as four subsidiary problems.

coming to the attention of the social worker to arise from the patient's own or his relatives' experience of physical or mental illness and disability. This proved not to be the case.

All episodes were classified as to whether or not the main problem was related to physical or mental illness or disability in the patient or his family. Some 30 per cent of all the main problems dealt with by the social worker were clearly connected with physical ill-health and a further 10 per cent with mental illness. On the other hand just over a third of the problems were in no way connected with illness or disability past or present, and in about a fifth of the episodes it was difficult to discern whether there was any connection between ill-health and the troubles brought to the social worker.

Some social problems were by their very nature closely associated with illness or disability, such as nearly all the requests for domiciliary services. Considerably fewer, just over half of the episodes in which patients were in the grip of a personal crisis, were closely associated with illness. A clear example was bereavement. However, 25 per cent of crisis episodes were not related to illness or disability. Examples are: panic before an academic examination or distress occasioned by a sudden separation from someone on whom the patient had depended a great deal, like a helpful neighbour who is rehoused. Less than half of the episodes in which family relationships were the main difficulty were related to illness or disability. A similar trend was observed where the main problem arose at work or at school or where there was financial need or housing difficulties.

In other words even when social work is carried out in the context of general practice a great deal of the social pathology dealt with arises from sources other than ill-health. When needs coming to the attention of the social worker were associated with illness or disability such situations were usually serious and chronic, such as malignancy, heart disease, after-effects of strokes or major surgery, and bronchitis.[1] Many of these patients were very old.

Patients and Problems
Did the problems the patients presented to their doctor and to the social worker differ in different age-groups, between men and women or according to the social class to which they belonged?

Clearly, different kinds of difficulties assail people at different

---

[1] This was confirmed by a retrospective analysis by the doctors, of a one-in-ten sample of patients who had complained of a physical illness to their doctor at the time of their referral to the social worker.

F

stages of their life. Thus school and vocational problems naturally predominated among the young. Problems associated with work were also prevalent among young people. Examples are: youngsters bored with dead-end jobs or flitting from job to job. Comparatively few work problems arose between the ages of 25 and 44 but 15 of the 42 patients with work difficulties were middle-aged or nearing their retirement. At this stage work problems can become intractable. If chronic illness or disability forces a man out of his customary employment in his mid-fifties, opportunities for retraining or alternative suitable employment are very limited.

Family problems understandably predominated between the ages of 25 and 44 when families grow and are exposed to the greatest amount of stress. Problems of material needs in relation to housing, money and domiciliary services increased dramatically with age. Over half (55 per cent) of the patients experiencing such needs were over the age of 65, and 20 per cent were aged 80 and over.

We also observed sex differences in the presentation of problems. For example, while equal proportions of men and women presented marital difficulties, parent/child problems were predictably more often the concern of women. Work problems occurred more often among men. Proportionately more men than women had personality difficulties, were suffering from mental illness or experienced difficulties with wider social relationships. A number of these men were middle-aged, of indifferent health, who lived an isolated existence in bed-sitting rooms and hostels. Men also presented proportionately twice as many psychiatric problems to the doctors in their interviews preceding referral as did women (15 per cent compared with 7 per cent). Numbers are very small and dictate caution but these findings are in contrast to prevalence studies of psychiatric morbidity in general practice (Shepherd et al. 1966), where usually more women than men suffer from psychiatric symptoms. One could speculate that men in the younger age-groups who had personality difficulties or who were suffering from mental illness were more likely to be referred to the social worker than women of similar age, particularly mothers of young families who may have been in touch with the health visitors attached to the practice.

A greater proportion of married, divorced and separated people had family difficulties than did single patients. The widowed, who included many elderly women who had been widowed for a long time, as well as the recently bereaved had proportionately more material problems and experienced more anxiety and personal crises. Single people presented work problems three times as often as the married, widowed and divorced. Over a quarter of the single patients (27 per cent) were either mentally ill or had personality difficulties or difficulties in wider social relationships, while these problems only applied to 10 per cent of the married patients, with the widowed and divorced falling approximately in the middle. This relationship between marital state and mental ill-health has been noted in other studies of psychiatric morbidity. Such findings have led to the age-old argument whether marriage is a protection against psychiatric illness and emotional difficulties or whether it is the mentally healthier who are more likely to marry.

Nearly half the patients belonging to the professional and managerial class revealed family difficulties as their main problem, and two-thirds of these were associated with marital stress. In contrast, less than a quarter (23 per cent) of patients in semi- and unskilled occupations presented family problems as their main difficulty. This trend was also observed in the ways in which the patients presented their difficulties to the doctors. It appears that the Caversham patients in the professional, managerial and white-collar occupations used the practice more as a source of direct help with family difficulties than did those in manual and unskilled occupations, who possibly were more familiar with the welfare agencies in the area and more ready to consult them.

A contrasting social class trend emerged in relation to problems connected with mental ill-health. Nearly a quarter of patients in semi- and unskilled occupations presented personality difficulties, mental illness and difficulties in wider social relationships as their main problems, while this only applied to 15 per cent of those in the professional and managerial classes, clerical and skilled manual workers falling in the middle. Possibly the professional classes more readily sought consultation with psychiatric specialists; or this concentration of mental ill-health in the lower social classes may reflect some form of downward social drift, particularly among those with chronic psychiatric illness (Goldberg and Morrison 1963).

As expected, only a small proportion of patients in professional and managerial jobs revealed environmental problems as their main difficulty, while one-fifth of those in semi- and unskilled occupations presented environmental difficulties, such as financial need, housing problems or needs for domiciliary services.

There was a clear link between the size of household and the main problems revealed. The larger the household, the greater the number of family problems there were likely to be. Nearly half the patients who lived in households containing four or more people presented stresses in family relationships as their predominant worry. A contrasting trend was observed in problems concerned with personality difficulties, mental illness and community relationships. These difficulties increased in frequency as the size of household declined—proportionately more people living alone experienced such problems. Small households consisting of one or two people also presented proportionately more financial and housing needs and required more domiciliary services than big households. As we have already seen, many of these one-person households consisted of elderly people living alone or of students and young professional people. The frequency of anxiety and crisis situations appeared to be independent of the size of household.

Summary
The majority of patients who were referred to the social worker presented vague psychosomatic complaints, emotional ill-health and overt social problems in their surgery consultations preceding the referral.

About a third of the problems revealed to the social worker were associated with emotional ill-health of some kind, with anxieties about health and with crisis situations; a third were related to difficulties in family relationships and a fifth of the problems were connected with material and environmental needs. Over half the patients discussed their main problems in their first interview with the social worker.

The patients' problems were associated with their age, sex, marital state and social class: material needs predominated among the elderly; family problems were more often the concern of women and were more frequently presented by patients belonging to the professional and managerial classes who may have shied away from using 'welfare' agencies; emotional ill-health was more concentrated among men, the single, those living alone and among patients in semi- and unskilled occupations.

REFERENCES

GOLDBERG, E. M. and MORRISON, S. L. (1963), 'Schizophrenia and Social Class', *Brit. J. Psychiat.* 109, (785–802).

7

THE SOCIAL WORK—PLAN AND ACTION

Social caseworkers often find it difficult to commit themselves to an explicit assessment of their clients' problems and they shy away even more from the formulation of treatment goals and methods. Much social work is based on intuition, empathy and exploration, following the client through all kinds of mazes and not infrequently getting lost with him. Hence it seemed to us important in this demonstration project not only to define the client population and assess its problems systematically but also to delineate treatment plans and to relate these to the action that followed. This exercise enabled us to observe how realistic plans had been and whether there emerged any typical ways of helping which had particular relevance to the general practice setting. We could also begin to ask whether different kinds of clients, the old, the young, the manual worker, the professional person had different kinds of help or whether there was no demonstrable relationship between age, sex or social characteristics of clients and the type of treatment received. Most important for the development of policy in social work, we hoped to discover whether patients who had social work treatment within the general practice setting differed from those who were referred to other agencies in the community for social work help. We might then be able to distinguish between the kinds of patients who needed to be helped in close collaboration with their general practitioners—under the roof, as it were, of general practice— and those who could be helped equally well in social work agencies.

Plan of Action
Wherever possible we formulated a treatment plan after the first interview. This was not intended to be a rigid prescription from which the social worker could not deviate, for clearly in changeable human situations unforeseen developments demanded a flexible approach.

We identified five broad categories of possible action (Table 7.1).

1 Clarification, assessment, advice and information.
2 Casework in the practice.
3 Referral to other agencies.
4 Further exploration.
5 Other.

Table 7.1

INITIAL PLAN OF SOCIAL WORK ACTION

Plan	Episodes* No.	%
1 Clarification, assessment, advice and information	103	10
2 Casework in the practice:		
Short-term	229	22
Long-term	38	4
3 Referral to other agencies	264	26
4 Further exploration	374	37
5 Other (i.e. Old Persons' Register)†	10	1
Not stated	2	—
Total	1020	100

* Totals may not always agree from table to table due to varying numbers of people for whom information is complete. Where appropriate, percentages have been rounded to nearest whole number and adjusted so that they add to 100.
† For description of Old Persons' Register see Chapter 2 page 25.

In a small proportion, 103 (10 per cent) of the 1,020 episodes in which the social worker had face-to-face contact with the client, clarification and assessment of the situation or simple advice and information only seemed to be required (category 1). The intention in these situations was to take no further action, or to refer the patient back to the doctor, or to leave the case open for the patient to return if he wished.[1]

In only 10 of these episodes was simple advice or information— such as telling someone how to apply for supplementary benefit— thought to be sufficient. It is worth remembering that the doctors were knowledgeable about local facilities, and that the secretary, receptionist and nurse also knew a great deal about the resources available in the area.

The remaining 93 episodes in category 1 were almost equally divided between those 44 episodes where patients were referred back to the doctor and those where initiative for any further interview was left to the patient (49 episodes).

Handing back to the doctor was thought to be appropriate when

[1] An account of clarification, assessment, advice and information will be found in Chapter 8.

patients were worried about the nature of the medical treatment prescribed, for instance, the implications of a diagnosis they did not fully understand. Clearly what the patient in these circumstances wanted was to talk to the doctor. The social worker sometimes was able to help the patient to reformulate his difficulties so that he could discuss them more coherently with his doctor. Other patients, though they may have had a social problem were really seeking the attention of the doctor. This applied especially to patients with long-standing physical ailments which they could manage with the occasional support of the doctor. Such a patient might interpret a referral to a social worker as a rejection by his general practitioner.

Occasionally a patient was referred who was quite unaware of any difficulties. If both the patient and those near him felt that things were going sufficiently well it seemed unwise to upset an equilibrium which, though possibly answering a pathological need, suited the patient and those around him. In other cases the social worker decided to refer the patient back to the doctor because specialist medical or psychiatric treatment appeared to be more appropriate than social work.

In 49 episodes the social worker, having clarified the situation with the patient in the first interview suggested that the next move should be his. For instance, a client might be doubtful whether or not to seek help, and consultation with his family might be one way of arriving at a decision. Some situations, though causing discomfort and unhappiness, did not seem bad enough for the patient to take action. Things had to become worse before the patient could bring himself to take action and face possible change. Other patients wanted to wait a while to see whether things might get better of their own accord. Occasionally these patients returned reporting improvement, at other times they decided that help was needed to bring about some change. Leaving the next move to the client is particularly appropriate in general practice where there are a number of other people he can turn to and where the door is permanently open. This is not necessarily so in social service agencies.

In 26 per cent of the episodes the social worker decided to take the patient on for casework treatment herself (category 2). In most of these episodes (22 per cent) the casework was expected to be of a short-term nature, lasting no more than three months.[1] In only 4 per cent of the episodes was a more open-ended and long-term contact visualised.[2]

---

[1] An account of short-term work will be found in Chapter 9.
[2] An account of long-term work will be found in Chapter 10.

The kind of cases for which short-term treatment within the practice seemed indicated were often crises affecting patients who usually coped well with their lives and where quick action was essential. Short-term help also seemed appropriate when patients expressed anxiety about their health and were continuing to receive treatment from their general practitioner. In this way their social and medical problems could be treated as a whole.

Referral to another agency for help was thought to be a suitable course of action in 26 per cent of the episodes (category 3). Such a plan might entail several interviews both with the patient and his family to clarify specific needs so that the appropriate service could be selected and approached on his behalf. It also often involved a good deal of preparatory work, both with the patients and with the agency.[1] Referral was intended in nearly half the episodes where the main need was for domiciliary services. Enlisting the help of another agency, usually a psychiatric clinic or the mental-health service of the local authority Health Department, was also the plan of choice in about half the episodes in which personality problems and mental illness were the main difficulties.

Referring patients to other agencies was not a matter of 'passing the buck', but clearly, as we have said, the social worker could not have accepted everyone, even for assessment, had she not been able to use other facilities in the community. Nor did she necessarily possess the specialised skills to work, for example, with certain types of psychiatric patients and their families. Indeed, she would have deprived patients of the most appropriate services available, had she planned to help them by herself.

There was, finally, a large group of patients (37 per cent) in which the social worker felt further exploration was needed before any plan of action could be formulated. This applied particularly to difficult marital situations and usually entailed several interviews.

Number of Interviews and Visits
When we now examine what help these patients and their families actually received we observe (Table 7.2) that in a quarter of the episodes simple assessment and clarification took place or advice and information were given. In 28 per cent of the episodes patients were referred to other agencies and in over two-fifths of the episodes (42 per cent) patients were taken on for short- or long-term casework within the practice.

[1] An account of the work with other agencies will be found in Chapter 11.

Table 7.2

NUMBER OF CONTACTS AND ACTION TAKEN

*Number of contacts**

Action taken	1		2		3		4		5–9		10 and over		Total	
	No.	%	No.	%	No.	%	No.	%	No.	%	No.	%	No.	%
Clarification, assessment, advice and information	104	51	64	34	34	22	13	25	18	8	4	3	273	25
Casework in practice	12	6	32	17	65	42	18	35	160	74	109	84	396	42
Referral to outside agencies	85	41	84	44	47	30	17	33	29	13	8	6	269	28
Other	5	2	10	5	10	6	4	7	11	5	9	7	48	5
All episodes	206	100	190	100	156	100	52	100	217	100	130	100	951	100

* A contact denotes either an interview at the practice or a visit outside the practice.

These figures only apply to those clients who had face-to-face contact with the social worker. It will be remembered that she did not see one-third of the patients referred to her, but often carried out a good deal of work on behalf of the clients she did not see. For instance, she would discuss the situation of clients who were in contact with other agencies with the social worker concerned and agree on a plan of action. On many occasions she arranged a case discussion between the social workers dealing with the case and the patient's doctor. In other instances, although the patient was not seen, the relatives were interviewed.

Four-fifths (821) of the patients seen had fewer than ten interviews per episode, nearly two-thirds (604) had between one and four contacts and about a fifth (217) had between five and nine contacts (Table 7.2). Only a small proportion, 14 per cent (130) had ten or more contacts per episode.

Looking at the length of contact in 74 per cent of the episodes the contact lasted for three months or less, and in 38 per cent it was under one month. At the other extreme, in 8 per cent of the episodes patients were in continuous contact between six and twelve months and in 1 per cent (10 episodes) for over a year. This clearly demonstrates that the majority of patients were short-term cases.

If we relate the number of contacts to the social work action taken, assessment or advice and referral to other agencies clearly demanded fewer contacts than casework treatment. However, it is worth noting that in over a quarter of the episodes in which assessment or advice was given patients had three or more contacts with the social worker. Cases in which referral to another agency took place also often involved more than one contact. Indeed, 38 per cent of the patients referred to another agency for advice and help had three or more contacts with the social worker at the practice.

Plan and Action
Comparing the treatment plan with what actually happened, we find considerable discrepancies, particularly where a referral to another agency was planned (Table 7.3). Only just over half of these 264 episodes were in fact referred; over a quarter (28 per cent) were taken on for casework and 11 per cent were only assessed or given information and advice. Many factors played a part in this apparently poor prediction. Some cases where the assessment interview indicated need for long-term help and support, and which the social worker intended to refer for these reasons, improved against all expectations. The

Table 7.3

PLAN OF SOCIAL WORK AND ACTION TAKEN

Plan of Social Work

Action taken	Clarification, assessment, advice and information		Casework in the practice		Referral to outside agencies		Other (i.e. Old persons' register)		Total planned		Exploration	
	No.	%	No.	%	No.	%	No.	%	No.	%	No.	%
Clarification, assessment, advice and information	69	67	29	11	29	11	4	40	131	20	119	32
Casework in practice	20	19	195	73	74	28	0	0	291	45	143	38
Referral to outside agencies	13	13	28	10	145	55	3	30	189	29	97	26
Other, not stated, not known	1	1	15	6	16	6	3	30	35	6	15	4
All episodes	103	100	267	100	264	100	10	100	646	100	374	100

opportunity to talk about their problems to a sympathetic listener seemed to have started a therapeutic process which referral to another agency would have interrupted. In some instances it proved impossible to fit problem and agency, particularly during the years preceding the reorganisation of the social services, when criteria for eligibility could be very rigid; on other occasions waiting lists deterred referrals and in yet other cases the patients, feeling at home and helped by the social worker in the practice, did not want to transfer to another agency.

Table 7.3 shows that plan and action were more highly correlated in those episodes in which casework in the practice was planned. In almost three-quarters of the episodes this intention was carried out; the other patients were able to manage, once their problems had been discussed and clarified, or they did not continue after the initial interviews or were referred to other agencies which seemed more appropriate to their needs. For example, the social worker had planned to work with a mother whose marriage had recently broken down. It soon emerged that in addition to her own problems her teenage daughter had difficulties. This family was referred to the Children's Department, where the adolescent could have her own worker if necessary.

In the 103 episodes in which clarification, assessment, advice and information were thought to be appropriate the plan worked fairly well, two-thirds were dealt with in this way, another fifth required casework and a small proportion (13 per cent) were referred to other agencies.

Finally we have to consider the social work action in the large proportion of episodes in which the social worker could not commit herself to any definite plan after her first interview and felt the need to explore further. As Table 7.3 indicates, the different types of action show a similar distribution to those for the planned cases. Of the episodes which needed further exploration 38 per cent were taken on for casework—compared with 45 per cent among the planned episodes; 26 per cent were referred—compared with the 29 per cent planned; a somewhat higher proportion of the exploratory episodes were only assessed or were given advice and information (32 per cent compared with 20 per cent). This was partly due to the greater uncertainty these clients felt about their need for social help and hence their greater tendency to discontinue contact.

On the whole, the social worker overestimated the number of patients she would refer to other agencies for treatment. One of the reasons for this was the difficulty she experienced in referring her clients to other social work agencies. But as we shall show, she also seemed to have changed her practice over the years. Another factor which made early planning difficult was that the social worker felt the need for further exploration in such a large proportion of her cases. The implications of this will be discussed in the concluding chapter.

Changes in Social Work Methods

If we compare the action taken by the social worker in the early and later stages of the project we observe considerable differences (Table 7.4). During the first six months, when the social worker was finding her bearings in general practice and the caseload was only beginning to build up, comparatively few cases were referred to other agencies. In 1966 and 1967 a higher proportion (over a third) were referred out. However, in 1968 the proportion of episodes taken on for casework in the practice grew to 59 per cent and those referred to other agencies dropped to 17 per cent; similarly, episodes in which assessment and advice was given decreased to 17 per cent.

There are several possible explanations for this apparent change in methods of working. While preparing an interim report on the project early in 1968 it became clear that the social worker was classifying as clarification and assessment many cases in which her work had a definite therapeutic purpose and amounted to short-term casework. There is little doubt that as a result of this report she subsequently changed her criteria of classification for category 1 (Table 7.4). These changes in criteria do not explain the drop in referrals to other agencies in 1968 and 1969. Here other factors may be at work. The number of self-referrals increased greatly during the latter years and the number of clients who were coming back for a third, fourth and fifth time also grew disproportionately. These were often patients with chronic and intractable problems, who had been referred to other agencies but preferred to come back to the social worker in the general practice. The social worker on her part had lost some of her early enthusiasm for referring patients to other social workers, as she discovered that some agencies interpreted their functions rather narrowly and were hesitant to accept and keep in touch with cases in which there was no obvious crisis.

It is also our impression that because of cumulative pressures on the social worker and because she felt pushed and busy she tended to discourage referrals to other agencies. It was sometimes easier and quicker to help clients within the practice, especially if the problem was of a short-term crisis nature, than to search for a suitable facility in the community, discuss the case with the social workers concerned

Table 7.4

DATE OF REFERRAL AND ACTION TAKEN

(Percentage distributions)

Action taken	*Date of referral*						
	1965 July–Dec.	*1966 Jan.–Dec.*	*1967 Jan.–Dec.*	*1968 Jan.–Dec.*	*1969 Jan.–June*	*July 1965 June 1969*
Clarification, assessment, advice and information	31	27	27	17	20	24
Casework in practice	44	32	38	59	40	43
Referral to outside agencies	23	40	35	17	21	28
Other	2	1	0	7	19	5
Total %	100	100	100	100	100	100
Number	173	237	244	234	132	1020

and sometimes write a well thought out report for the agency. Also the doctors, who were getting more knowledgeable about the social services in the neighbourhood, were themselves referring more patients to outside agencies directly. Therefore the patients they referred to the practice social worker in the later months may have been those they wished her to take on herself.

Client Characteristics and Treatment

The next question we explored was whether the method of treatment varied in relation to the clients' social characteristics. For example, were the aged more frequently referred to other agencies? Was casework treatment more often undertaken with articulate clients from the managerial and white collar strata?

The type of action varied little in relation to the client's age. A small exception were those elderly clients who were not seen by the social worker. A greater proportion of them than of other clients were referred to other agencies. However, of those over sixty-five years of age who had personal contact with the social worker, the proportion referred to other agencies and taken on for casework is similar to that of younger age-groups. Even more unexpectedly, in view of other studies (Myers and Schaffer 1954, Goldberg 1955), methods of treatment did not vary according to the social class from which the client came. It had seemed reasonable to assume that the more sophisticated clients from the upper social classes would more often be taken on for casework which demanded some self-awareness and ability to verbalise, and that they would be referred less often to other social agencies than clients from semi- and unskilled occupations.

Although the methods of treatment were apparently not influenced by the clients' social class, the type of agency to which they were referred did show interesting variations in relation to the clients' social position. Proportionately more of the patients belonging to the semi- and unskilled occupational groups were referred to local authority departments (Children's, Health and Welfare), while proportionately more patients in the managerial and professional groups were referred to voluntary agencies such as the casework department of the Camden Council of Social Service, and also to hospital social workers and to psychiatric clinics. The explanation may be that since clients in the professional and managerial classes presented mainly psycho-social difficulties they tended to be referred to agencies which had expertise in these spheres. Working-class patients who often experienced both

Table 7.5

SOCIAL CLASS AND NUMBER OF CONTACTS

(Percentage distributions)

No. of Interviews	Social class*			
	I and II	III *non-manual*	III *manual*	IV and V
Less than 5 interviews	59	55	52	43
More than 5 interviews	41	45	48	57
Total %	100	100	100	100
Number	158	175	153	176

* In this and the following table, the figures represent all *persons* seen by the social worker excluding those who could not be classified by social class. For these comparisons we used the Registrar General's social class classification rather than socio-economic groupings.

material and psycho-social problems needed the help of agencies with appropriate resources to meet these needs.

There are other indications that the kind of help received differed in relation to social class. A small but consistent social class trend can be observed in relation to the number of interviews clients had (Table 7.5). Those in social classes I and II had fewest, and patients

Table 7.6

SOCIAL CLASS AND NUMBER OF EPISODES PER PATIENT

No. of episodes per patient	Social Class								All classes	
	I and II		III *non-manual*		III *manual*		IV and V			
	N	%	*N*	%	*N*	%	*N*	%	*N*	%
1	122	77	121	69	105	69	107	61	455	69
2 and 3	34	22	48	27	45	29	60	34	187	28
4 and 5	2	1	6	4	3	2	9	5	20	3
Total	158	100	175	100	153	100	176	100	662*	100

* This figure represents all *persons* seen by the social worker excluding those who could not be classified by social class.

Table 7.7

MAIN PROBLEM AND ACTION TAKEN

Action taken	Main problem													
	Problems in family relationships		Problem at work, school		Financial need, housing problems, need for domiciliary services		Anxiety about health, personal crisis		Psychiatric illness, personality difficulties, problems in social relationships		Others/Not known		Total	
	No.	%	No.	%	No.	%	No.	%	No.	%	No.	%	No.	%
Clarification, assessment, advice and information	72	24	31	31	36	19	38	20	41	23	32	46	250	24
Casework in practice	122	40	46	47	74	40	99	53	78	45	15	21	434	43
Referral to outside agencies	99	33	18	18	67	36	40	22	45	26	17	24	286	28
Other	10	3	4	4	10	5	9	5	11	6	6	9	50	5
Totals	303	100	99	100	187	100	186	100	175	100	70	100	1020	100

G

in social classes IV and V had most. This is also reflected in the number of episodes of social work treatment. Just over three-quarters (77 per cent) of the clients in social classes I and II had only one episode of social work help, while this applied to just under two-thirds (61 per cent) of clients in social classes IV and V (Table 7.6), social class III falling neatly in the middle. Conversely, only 22 per cent of the clients in social classes I and II had two or more spells of social work help compared with 39 per cent in social classes IV and V.

Thus it seems that clients who experienced most troubles also received most help.

Main Problem and Social Work Action
The method of treatment did not vary markedly according to the main problems revealed (Table 7.7), though there were a few exceptions: proportionately more patients who found themselves in the throes of a personal crisis, or who were anxious about their health, received casework in the practice. On the other hand, about half the episodes in which there was a specific need for the provision of services were referred to other agencies. In most other problem categories between a fifth and a quarter of the episodes were dealt with by clarification, assessment or advice, about two-fifths by casework in the practice, and between a quarter and a third were referred to other agencies.

Similarly the amount of action, as reflected in the number of contacts the social worker had with the clients and their families, did not vary much in relation to the main problem area (Table 7.8). It will be seen that in practically all problem categories over half the episodes (about 60 per cent) had less than five interviews, between 20 per cent and 25 per cent had between five and nine interviews. Small differences between problem areas can be detected where the social worker had more than ten contacts. We have already mentioned that in over half the episodes in which a crisis or anxiety about health were the main problem the social worker engaged in casework, and this is reflected in the comparatively high proportion (19 per cent) of the episodes which involved more than ten interviews (Table 7.8). Clients whose problems related to personality and mental illness had rather more interviews than patients with other kinds of main problems. As we shall see later, the social worker experienced considerable difficulties in trying to find the right kind of treatment agencies for patients with chronic personality problems or psychiatric disabilities.

While the type of main problems did not appear to exert great influence on the kind of action taken nor on the amount of time spent

Table 7.8

MAIN PROBLEM AND NUMBER OF CONTACTS

(percentage distributions)

Number of contacts	Main problem					
	Problems in family relationships	Problem at work, school	Financial need, housing problems, need for domiciliary services	Anxiety about health, personal crisis	Psychiatric illness, personality difficulties, problems in social relationships	Others/Not known
1	18	18	23	22	15	36
2	18	27	14	18	19	16
3	14	19	21	10	17	10
4	7	4	6	4	3	1
5–9	21	21	22	24	22	14
10 or more	15	5	7	19	18	3
Not known	7	6	7	3	6	20
Total %	100	100	100	100	100	100
Number	303	99	187	186	175	70

Table 7.9
NUMBER OF SUBSIDIARY PROBLEMS AND ACTION TAKEN

Action taken	Number of subsidiary problems											
	0		1		2		3		4		Total	
	No.	%	No.	%	No.	%	No.	%	No.	%	No.	%
Clarification, assessment, advice and information	33	38	61	31	95	23	23	19	21	19	233	25
Casework in practice	24	28	70	35	181	43	60	50	59	52	394	42
Referral to agencies	25	39	55	28	128	30	29	24	31	27	268	28
Others	5	5	12	27	17	4	10	7	2	2	46	5
Totals	87	100	198	100	421	100	122	100	113	100	941	100

with clients, the complexity of the problems did. Table 7.9 shows clearly that the more problems clients experienced the greater the involvement of the social worker. In over half (52 per cent) of the episodes in which there were four or more subsidiary problems clients were taken on for casework, as compared with only 28 per cent of the episodes in which clients had no subsidiary problems. The converse is true of assessment and advice: the fewer the problems the more this short method of disposal was used. In contrast, the proportion of referrals to other agencies as a main mode of treatment did not vary appreciably with the number of subsidiary problems clients had. It may be asked why only a quarter of those who experienced many difficulties were referred to other agencies. Possibly two factors were at work here. General practice often serves as a containing net for people who have many and intractable problems. The door of general practice is always open and often the case goes no further. On the other hand, many social workers still divide their clientele into helpable 'hopeful' cases, namely those who respond to social work methods aimed at a change in attitudes or relationships, and the other kind—those who do not. Many of the patients with multiple problems which are often a mixture of health, environmental and psycho-social problems do not respond to these methods (Mayer and Timms 1970). Thus, referral to other casework agencies was not easy in these cases, or indeed appropriate. The aims of social work support for these clients within the practice were modest. The social worker tried to

Table 7.10

NUMBER OF SUBSIDIARY PROBLEMS AND NUMBER OF CONTACTS

(Percentage distributions)

Total number of contacts	Number of subsidiary problems					
	0	1	2	3	4	*Total*
0	1	1	—	—	—	—
1	48	31	19	11	5	22
2	21	27	21	15	12	20
3	12	17	19	16	11	17
4	5	4	5	7	7	5
5–9	12	18	22	28	36	23
10 or more	1	2	14	23	29	13
Total %	100	100	100	100	100	100
Number	87	198	421	122	113	941

help them and their families over crises, quite aware that their basic difficulties would not be affected by this.

Another way of looking at the same phenomenon is to compare the number of contacts the social worker had with clients with the number of subsidiary problems that were detected. Table 7.10 shows a significant association between the number of subsidiary problems and the number of contacts the social worker had with clients and their families. In those episodes in which no subsidiary problems or only one was revealed, 3 per cent of the patients had ten or more interviews; this proportion rises steadily with the number of subsidiary problems, so that 29 per cent of the patients experiencing four or more subsidiary problems had ten or more interviews. One could offer two diverging explanations for these findings. First, that those who had the greatest need for help received most, or conversely that the social worker detected most problems among those with whom she had prolonged contact.

In the next chapter we shall give a more detailed description of the kind of work the social worker undertook, and although we lack quantitative documentation, it is our impression that she did give more time to those who had manifold problems to begin with and that the detection of their difficulties was not to any great extent the result of her intensive work with them.

It seems then that in this sample of social work clients in general practice, their age, sex and social characteristics had little effect on the method of treatment adopted. Nor could this analysis of discrete factors, such as age, sex, social class and main problem discriminate between those patients who needed to be helped within the practice and those who could equally well be referred to social service agencies. (Possibly an analysis which could have picked out the *configuration* of both main and subsidiary problems, and related these to the medical situation might have shown more differences.) Our material indicated that crisis situations could be speedily and effectively tackled in the practice. It also appeared that the more complex and chronic the problems, the more likely they were to be dealt with in the practice. This finding may be a comment on the accessibility of the social worker in general practice in contrast to the relative inaccessibility of the social services, rather than an indication that these types of clients needed treatment within the practice setting.

Circumstances of Closure
This project was not designed to evaluate the outcome of social work

in general practice. Since we could not find any ready-made objective criteria for assessing the outcome of social work, we were content with a simple classification of reasons for closure, a classification which had been found useful among clients of the London Family Welfare Association. As Table 7.11 shows, in ninety-nine of the episodes (10 per cent) the patients ceased to come, that is to say they discontinued without the explicit agreement of the social worker. A high proportion of these patients dropped out after assessment or clarification. This applied particularly to patients who had complained of vague psychosomatic symptoms in the first place. It is possible that some patients who chose the 'somatic' language for their difficulties were not ready to explore underlying psycho-social problems.

Secondly, the case may have been closed because both patient and social worker agreed that this was the best course to take. Table 7.11 shows that over half of these patients had received casework in the practice. On the whole our impression is that mutual decision to end the contact indicated improvement and a feeling that the client could now manage on his own.

Thirdly, in a small proportion of the episodes the social worker decided that the contacts should be discontinued. This often happened early on at the clarification and assessment stage. As we have discussed earlier in this chapter, occasionally the social worker felt that the problems referred to her really belonged to the doctor or that other specialists, particularly psychiatrists in cases of mental ill-health, would be more able to help. At times the social worker encountered interpersonal relationships in which searching discussions could have stirred up more problems than a social worker could have coped with.

Fourthly, cases were closed because clients were referred to another agency. This happened in over two-fifths of the episodes. Here we should note that in addition to those episodes in which referral was the main method of treatment, one hundred and forty-eight (15 per cent) of all episodes were referred to another agency after they had received casework treatment in the practice. (See Table 7.11.) As we shall describe in more detail in Chapter 9 many patients needed help of a personal kind within the practice before they were ready to accept social help elsewhere, or a crisis had to be dealt with straight away before clients could be handed on for help with other continuing social problems.

Finally, a small proportion of clients finished their contacts either because they moved or because death intervened.

Table 7.11

ACTION TAKEN AND REASON FOR CLOSURE

Reason for closure	Action taken								All episodes	
	Clarification, assessment, advice and information		Casework in practice		Referral to outside agencies		Other			
	No.	%	No.	%	No.	%	No.	%	No.	%
Patient stopped	68	28	20	5	9	3	2	10	99	10
Mutual decision	102	42	182	45	17	6	5	24	306	32
Social worker's decision	32	13	19	5	9	3	2	10	62	7
Referral	25	10	148	36	238	84	11	52	422	44
Moved, died or other	16	7	38	9	10	4	1	4	65	7
Total	243	100	407	100	283	100	21	100	954	100

Summary

Comparing the social worker's treatment-plan with the work she actually carried out we found that she had overestimated the number of cases she would be able to refer to other agencies. Over the four years she took on 43 per cent of the 1,020 episodes for casework treatment which usually lasted under three months and involved less than ten interviews. The proportion of cases referred to social service agencies dropped considerably during the last two years of the project. The type of social work action—assessment, casework in the practice, or referral—did not vary markedly in relation to the clients' age, social class or the kinds of problems they were experiencing. However, clients in the semi- and unskilled occupations had more interviews than those in the higher social classes and they came back for help more often. We also found that the more problems clients had the more likely it was they would receive casework in the practice, and the greater the number of contacts they were likely to have with the social worker.

No objective evaluation of outcome was attempted but the reasons for closing cases gave some indication of the state of affairs at the end of an episode.

REFERENCES

GOLDBERG, E. M. *et al.* (1968), 'Social Work in General Medical Practice', *Lancet*, *ii*, (552–5).

GOLDBERG, E. M. (1955), 'Some Developments in Professional Collaboration and Research in the U S A', *Brit. J. Psychiat., Soc. Work, 3.*

HOLLINGSHEAD, A. and REDLICH, F. (1958), *Social Class and Mental Illness: a Community Study.* New York, Wiley.

MAYER, J. E. and TIMMS, N. (1970), *The Client Speaks.* London, Routledge & Kegan Paul.

MYERS, J. K. and SCHAFFER, L. (1954), 'Social Stratification and Psychiatric Practice', *Amer. Sociol. Rev. 19* (307–10).

PART III

SOCIAL WORK IN ACTION

8

CLARIFICATION, ASSESSMENT, INFORMATION AND ADVICE

So far we have related social work to the broad characteristics of the clients and their circumstances. Now we will try to convey what the social worker actually did in response to particular situations and how she adapted her methods to the demands and stimulus of a general practice setting.[1]

As we showed in Chapter 7 (Table 7.2), in 237 episodes the course of action taken by the social worker consisted of clarification, assessment, information or advice. Obviously these activities cannot be sharply separated, for in various combinations they form an intrinsic part of all social work practice. In 182 episodes a patient received brief help from the social worker and the initiative for further contact was left to him. In another 68 episodes the patient primarily needed further medical treatment from his doctor or a referral by him to a medical colleague. Realising this, the social worker referred the patient back to the doctor.

Leaving the Initiative to the Client
General practitioners leave the initiative for further contact with their patients for much of the time, for the door of the practice is open, the staff are accessible and patients know they are expected to return if difficulties recur, or if the prescribed treatment fails to relieve their situation. Where the social worker was confident that patients would unhesitatingly return to see her if the need arose, she similarly left the initiative for further interviews with them, especially when information and advice was all that was immediately required. Giving information is an essential part of social work in any setting; in general practice it involved giving information to the social worker's patients and also to other members of the practice team. All members of the practice were anxious that patients should know about facilities in the

[1] To reduce the risk of discussing only those cases which we remembered most vividly we selected a random one-in-ten sample of all patients referred and used these as case illustrations in Chapters 8, 9 and 10.

Borough which might prove helpful to them. They also considered that patients should be conversant with their rights as citizens over matters which affected them or their families. The social worker was often involved in seeking out accurate information to enable her colleagues to assist patients she may never have met herself and whose names did not appear on her formal caseload. The discussion of information, which happened continuously within the practice, inevitably increased the knowledge of members of the team as well as that of the patient.

With some of her clients the social worker found that practical assistance combined with sympathy and encouragement helped them with life's challenges. Academic examinations, planning a career, facing an illness or retirement can cause anxiety and a little help at the right time can prove effective. Patients who had been ill and had not worked for some time might feel apprehensive about starting work and need help with finding a job. For older people living alone prompt assistance during acute illness, like advice about how to apply for supplementary benefit, or information about domiciliary services could reassure them that help was available, both in the present and during a future dependent old age. Appropriate information and advice led to an observable improvement if it was given at a time when a patient was motivated to take action. One such patient, an active lady of sixty-seven, wrote to her general practitioner to say that she had retired and thought he should be informed. Subsequent conversation between this highly independent widow, her general practitioner and the social worker disclosed her anxiety that her life-long good health could not last; she viewed retirement apprehensively as a prelude to illness and inactivity. At this point of change she was glad to use information obtained by the social worker about leisure and holiday facilities to fill her newly acquired free time with interesting activity.

The social worker and her colleagues in the practice were frequently surprised how little patients knew about services available and how to make use of them. How to apply for a social security supplement, fill in a sickness benefit form, obtain a grant for a school uniform or free school meals, find social clubs in the Borough or avail themselves of other services which were provided under statute were all matters on which patients from all social classes and age-groups seemed relatively ill-informed. Similarly, there were often gaps in their knowledge of the rights and duties they had incurred through entering into legal contracts, ranging from marriage, to hire purchase or tenancy agreements. The help of the Citizen's Advice Bureau was often sought on these matters, for it was important that such information given to patients was accurate.

Information and practical assistance was also sought by patients who found it difficult to cope with the complexities of modern living. Among this group were mentally handicapped patients and immigrants who were unfamiliar both with the English language and with the forms they had to complete in their daily lives. For example, official letters about income tax or National Insurance benefits were often bewildering to these people because they could not understand the obscure language contained in them. Anybody in the practice was willing to help such patients fill in a form or offer a simple piece of advice. The general practice was sometimes the only place where this could be done easily, as it was near their homes, open all day and in the evening and staffed by people they knew.

Information and advice alone were not sufficient for other patients who required more detailed exploration of complex difficulties. In some of these instances the initiative for further interviews was left with the patient because a few discussions appeared to have given him a clearer understanding of his problem and its possible solutions, and it seemed likely that he would be able to take the next steps on his own or with his family's help. When a brief contact started the process of communication further intervention might even prove unhelpful, as the case of a young engaged couple illustrated. The girl, recently arrived in this country for her marriage, complained to her general practitioner about her depression and apathy. Her fiancé was bewildered and defensive for he thought her unhappiness was due to doubts about their marriage. In a joint interview, the patient used the social worker as a neutral third person through whom she described to her listening fiancé her upset at leaving her family and friends, her exhaustion after preparing for her journey and her nervousness about meeting new people. Her fiancé's attitude changed as he perceived the causes for her depression and realised the patience and affection she needed from him. At this point the social worker decided that there was no need for her to intervene further.

A similar, temporarily disabling effect was occasioned by other events, especially if they brought a wave of guilt. One old lady was unable to seek probate for her husband's will until she had told somebody about their many quarrels over money. The patient had to confess to some impartial stranger and experience reassurance before she could take action.

Family groups who were reluctant to engage in joint discussion of their problems elsewhere were sometimes willing to come together to see the social worker in the general practice. When social work or psychiatric treatment had failed, such families sometimes returned to their general practitioner for a reassessment of their situation and a decision about their next step, just as physically ill patients returned to him for advice if they felt that a period of hospital treatment had not benefitted them. Such a round-table discussion with the social worker was particularly appropriate where urgent problems necessitated a quick decision on which a family disagreed. For example, the parents of a child, so disturbed that she was about to be excluded from school, attacked the child guidance clinic and the school and denied that their child was anything but 'normal'. They refused to send her to a special school. Although both parents had been seen separately over the years there had never been a joint discussion. The father hoped his daughter would go to university; the mother was illiterate and considered education unimportant. It was clear that their conflict of views about the child and her schooling was having a serious effect on her. The general practice was the only place to which both parents were willing to come together. The practice social worker helped these parents sort out possible alternatives; when they decided to accept a place in a special school for their child the initiative for further interviews was left with them. It was correctly anticipated that their contact with the staff of the school and with the psychiatrist and social worker attached to it would prove helpful to them and to their daughter.

Clarification and assessment of the situation could also be a complex process when the care of elderly people was jeopardised by conflict in their family. Relatives who did not speak to each other would sometimes meet at the practice to discuss the old person's well-being, returning to their silent war after the interview was over. Disagreements were accepted but not explored by the social worker because the family were not seeking help on this basis. At least, these family confrontations showed the team who would be prepared to help, in what way and how much, for despite their conflicts, such families demonstrated their concern for the old person by coming to the discussions.

Difficulties in Assessment
Sometimes the process of assessment and clarification necessitated joint consultations not only with several members of the family but with people outside and within the practice team.

The most difficult decision for the social worker and the practice team was to refrain from intervening. The action needed might be clear, but the time inopportune. The team then had to wait for the right time, usually when the patient made a more definite request for assistance. These were anxious situations because such patients were often badly in need of help, but had to get worse before they could accept it. 'No action for the moment' was the decision about a young man who was seriously mentally ill and came to the social worker for legal advice. Although the general practitioner had wished to meet and treat this man for some time, this patient had never come to the surgery. The social worker gave him the advice he sought and introduced him informally to the rest of the team. This gave the young man an opportunity to 'size up' the practice staff. If medical treatment had been pressed upon him, he might have taken fright and disappeared. This approach paid dividends, for later he made an appointment with one of the doctors.

A decision about what advice should be given to a patient and by whom could also be difficult to make. For example, some patients asked for advice about the type of employment they should seek or continue. Occasionally, mental illness not amenable to treatment was revealed by patients in responsible jobs like hospital pharmacist, bus driver and teacher. In such cases the practice team had to consider the nature of the patient's symptoms and their effect on the people who were dependent upon him. The interest of the patient had to be reconciled with the interests of those for whom he was responsible. It would have been irresponsible of the practice to assume that the wishes of the patient always took priority. Should, for example, a paranoid and hallucinated coach driver be encouraged to carry on with his job?

Assessment of a patient's difficulties could also involve an appraisal by the practice team of their own reaction to this particular patient. For example, a bright attractive young woman had several children who were all inadequately fed and clothed and showing early signs of delinquency. Often she came with vague physical symptoms to her general practitioner as a prelude to demanding that he should 'do' something about the current crisis in her marriage. The way in which she presented her problem in the form of an acute crisis often engendered a panic over-reaction on the part of the general practitioner, in contrast to the calm response which usually prevailed with other patients. In discussion with the social worker this patient described the many female social workers with whom she was in

H

contact, and indicated that their efforts were deflated by her own
tendency to play workers off against each other and then convince
people like her male practitioner that nobody was 'doing anything'.
It was clear to all members of the team that this family needed social
work help badly; a concerted, unified effort to get hold of the problems
and cope with the mother's manipulation necessitated regular meetings
between the general practitioner and other social workers involved.
The practice social worker's role was to reassess the situation, bring
other social workers and the general practitioner together and,
occasionally, to oil the wheels of their continuing communication.
The doctor and the workers concerned agreed that a team of people
needed to work in unison with this family because their individual
problems were serious and the family relationships so competitive.
This plan apparently ran counter to the notion of reducing the number
of workers visiting a family, but it illustrates how some families with
diverse and severe difficulties may require a team of people working
in liaison.

Other social assessments led to painful conclusions. What was
wrong and what was needed might be clear, but lack of ability or of
resources might prevent effective help being given. For example, an
elderly and ill patient, living alone and wishing to remain at home
might be neglected because of inadequate domiciliary services or
become depressed if unwillingly admitted to hospital. The phrase 'if
he goes into hospital he may die' is all too commonly heard in general
practice. A social assessment which exposes lack of knowledge,
limitations in skill and gaps in the community services can increase
frustration, which spurs a team on to social action.

Patients Referred Back to their Doctor
On sixty-eight occasions the social worker and general practitioner
agreed that the patient who had been referred for social work help was
primarily needing or seeking further attention from his general
practitioner. In over half of these sixty-eight episodes the social
worker referred the patient back to their general practitioner because
she considered they might be mentally ill and needing psychiatric
treatment.

The overt symptoms which these patients had initially presented
often did not differ from those brought by other patients whose
difficulties were found to stem mainly from social problems with
which the social worker could help. These symptoms ranged from
depression, inability to concentrate and insomnia, to preoccupation

with thoughts about suicide or violence to others. Sometimes these signs were accompanied by other complaints such as impotence, frigidity, headaches or fear of a particular disease.

Depression was brought to general practice in many guises, in its classic form, or underlying apparent anxiety states. Seriously depressed patients often gave the well-known picture of being passive and withdrawn, with drooping shoulders, clutching on to their lap anything they carried, presenting their story in a monotonous monologue and not looking fully at the social worker until the end of their interview. A few patients did not keep further appointments, either with the general practitioner or with the social worker. This happened with a middle-aged widow who complained to her doctor of depression and made an incoherent request for legal advice for which she was referred to the social worker. She looked thin, apathetic and remote, and throughout her interview cried quietly, without apparent relief. Since her bereavement two years previously she said she had seldom been out of her home and now kept her only child away from school to keep her company. She came to see the doctor and the social worker once. When she did not keep further appointments it was concluded that this patient had used the social worker as a 'third ear' of her doctor, that she was desperate and without immediate help might even attempt suicide. Although the general practitioners did not usually visit patients without request, this patient's condition required such action. Her general practitioner visited her, treated her physical condition and referred her and her child to a psychiatrist. The social worker contributed to a fuller assessment process and subsequently explained the reasons for this child's non-attendance to the education welfare officers so that they would be ready to help in appropriate ways.

The needs of other depressed patients could be more difficult to assess, for the fear of mental illness meant that their problems were sometimes presented in other ways, perhaps anxiety over employment, perhaps brought to the doctor's notice by outsiders rather than by the patient himself. For example, a recently married young wife wrote to the general practitioner to say that she was worried because her husband was suddenly unable to keep his jobs. When seen by the social worker this acutely anxious young man was inarticulate, sweating profusely and despairing because since his marriage he had been impotent. The psychiatrist to whom the general practitioner referred this patient considered that this man had struggled with a severe depression for years, which had remained unrecognised by his parents and siblings. Florid symptoms had come to the surface through the sympathy of his young wife since his marriage. While this couple waited for psychiatric treatment, the social worker supported and reassured the wife which enabled her to comfort her husband.

Psychotic illnesses of patients were occasionally not apparent during initial interviews, especially if the patient was young, intelligent and produced a convincing intellectual explanation for his difficulties. A young man who complained to his doctor about depression and inability to find work was referred to the social worker for help to find a job. She observed in the first interview that he was neither depressed nor seeking work. It was only on his fourth visit that he revealed to her his fluctuating moods and hallucinations. The psychiatrist to whom the general practitioner referred this young man diagnosed schizophrenia. The social worker sometimes had further contact with these seriously ill patients and their families when they turned to the general practice for help in crises.

Sometimes it was difficult to assess whether an adolescent needed psychiatric help or not, for stormy but normal vocational, family and social problems could sometimes be difficult to distinguish from more pathological situations.

In less than half of the sixty-eight occasions on which patients were referred back to their doctor, they viewed their problem and its solution in purely somatic terms. This relatively small number of cases indicates the care with which the general practitioners tried to select patients with problems appropriate for a social worker's help. Occasionally a patient was referred to the social worker who had been too embarrassed or nervous to request further physical examination from the doctor. Sometimes a doctor who was aware of anxiety but could not discover its cause would ask the social worker for further exploration. A married woman who had complained vaguely to her doctor of her 'nerves' and infertility told the social worker she had hoped he might give her a vaginal examination and perhaps refer her on to a fertility clinic. The social worker helped her to voice this request to the doctor as quickly as possible, for the doubts of such patients about the relevance of social work were soon apparent.

Other patients presented physical symptoms which were familiar to their doctor because they had been extensively investigated over the years. These symptoms usually occurred at a time of stress and the patient responded to sympathy and palliative treatment. The general practitioner and social worker realised that the social and emotional problems of some of these patients arose from deep-rooted causes which were probably not accessible to social work help; in any case there might have been only minimal gains to the patient who usually coped with life reasonably well. In these cases doctor and social worker decided to restrict the length and degree of social work intervention which was offered. Occasionally, when the nature of the current crisis was unclear, such patients were referred to the social worker for assessment. Some were willing to see her indefinitely, but after a brief period of support and advice they were referred back to their doctor, although they could seek further interviews with the social worker if they wished. For example, the general practitioner and social worker decided that prolonged attention might increase the fear of a middle-aged widow who lived in fear of cancer for many years and during times of stress complained of a pain in her throat for which no physical cause could be found. The social worker kept in touch with her during the current crisis of her only son's marriage and then reinforced her doctor's advice that she should return to work. She was referred back to her general practitioner for a final certificate and encouragement to resume employment, for experience showed that her friendships at work supported her. In these cases it seemed that undue attention from the general practitioner or a social worker in his team could lead to an increase in anxiety rather than to any relief.

Other patients expected a physical cure from the doctor in the shortest possible time and were resentful if this involved even a minimal disruption of their lives. A middle-aged man, normally a wanderer, currently had a highly-paid casual job and came to the practice with extensive scabies. Angrily he resisted the doctor's directive that he should not work until this highly infectious disease was treated. He rejected the social worker's offer of practical help, but from the practice nurse he accepted clean second-hand clothes and responded to her encouragement to keep his hospital appointments. A medical 'iron hand in a velvet glove' was important to this man, and other patients like him, for while he argued with his masculine doctor, he obeyed the gentle but determined nurse.

With other patients, the social worker had no alternative but to leave the initiative for further interviews to them, either because they did not keep further appointments or because they refused any type of assistance. Among these patients were some young people with no fixed abode and few friends. Occasionally, it was possible to help these wanderers to accept hostel accommodation and obtain supplementary benefit. Some were addicted to drugs. A few accepted first-aid social help, others drifted through the practice attending the general practitioner for as long as they felt physically ill and then moved on. Sometimes these patients were highly suspicious of social workers but had limited trust in the general practitioner or in the practice nurse. While receiving medical treatment they would use her ability to listen sympathetically and give helpful advice.

Some older near-destitute people came to see the social worker. One woman, turned out of a hostel because of her fleas and smell carried all her worldly goods under countless layers of clothes but seemed to keep healthy and active. The patient was typical of a dozen or so other 'winter visitors' to the general practice. Their needs were basic—food, a warm place to sit and somewhere dry to sleep. Often they had already rejected or been rejected by the statutory and voluntary facilities which were first suggested by the social worker, and it was difficult to find them the material care they needed. Perhaps they demonstrated the need for a kind of community facility which is sufficiently flexible to cope with their many material and emotional problems, intimate enough to give them the companionship they sometimes seek, but not demanding that they give any more information about themselves than they choose to reveal. Without the care such patients get from organisations like the Salvation Army, their plight would be even more desperate.

Summary
Many different situations and problems were presented by patients who were not taken on for social work treatment, but whose difficulties were mainly assessed and clarified. These assessments and decisions could be comparatively straightforward when patients only needed a simple piece of advice, or they could be complex when multi-faceted family problems faced the team. For some patients social work help was not their first need, which was for medical care of various kinds; other patients were only able to accept first-aid help. For other patients the process of clarification of their troubles, sometimes combined with advice and encouragement, was sufficient to enable them to cope on their own. With these patients the door was left open for them to return if need be.

9

SHORT-TERM HELP

Short-term help by the social worker (up to twelve interviews in less than three months) was given in 286 episodes. Its aims were usually to help patients cope with some aspect of their current situation, like their employment, leisure or some family difficulty. In order to understand the present it was often necessary to know something about past events. Patients talked about their past experiences with the social worker and gained the relief which this often afforded, but the social worker consistently tried to direct attention towards the present, so that some practical plan could emerge. As we have stressed before, patients often presented a cluster of inter-related problems. For the sake of clarity we shall describe the social work carried out in relation to a number of main problem areas which seemed to influence the ways initial help was given.

Cultural Problems
Difficulties associated with the ethnic origin of patients arose continuously in the setting of general practice. To recent immigrants speaking little English, illness and the health service could be bewildering experiences. The doctors and other practice staff tried to explain diagnosis and treatment to these people and the receptionist would always be willing to help them complete the unfamiliar and complicated forms required for obtaining their sickness benefit. Problems arose from their attitudes towards medical tests and treatment, attitudes which were strange to Western medical and social practitioners. One patient, for example, was particularly worried when she learnt that a sample of her blood was to be sent away to hospital for analysis. It was some weeks before the general practitioner and social worker understood that to this patient the possession of her blood implied possession of power over her. Although she was intelligent and well educated, her fear of blood-tests and her illness reawakened attitudes which were deeply embedded in her culture of origin. Once these were understood, her apparently irrational be-

haviour could be accepted and she could be helped towards a more realistic understanding of the medical procedures. These different attitudes to medical treatment needed to be recognised, for a doctor or a social worker may be invested with many kinds of authority in the eyes of the patient and these may give even chance remarks unintended meanings.

The social problems of some patients stemmed partly from conflict between two different cultures, and the social worker could never assume that her terms of reference were those of the patient. The very role of a social worker might be foreign to such patients and an explanation of what a social worker tries to do was worthwhile.

'The doctor believes that sometimes illness can bring worry and that worry can bring illness. I am here as part of the practice team to try to help with these worries. Some people find this helpful, others not.' When the social worker could not understand the patient's point of view she would say 'I am sorry, I know you do things differently at home—would you mind explaining?'

The patient's description provided information and understanding about what change had meant.

Problems referred to the social worker included difficulties arising from racial differences, attitudes towards marriage of patients from Eastern countries, towards abortion of patients from Catholic countries and towards leprosy in the case of a woman from Pakistan. Problems arising from culture clash were not confined to people born outside Britain. The duties and status within a Muslim community might be easier to discern than the cultural differences between groups in a local school or housing estate.

In the following example, the social worker's job was to understand different values, see their repercussions on the patient and find some solution to bridge the gap between an inherited Eastern way of thinking and that of the Western culture in which he was living. A young man rejected his doctor's advice to return to work because he had 'a terrible pain around his heart'. He told the social worker that he came from a wealthy Indian family, and was sent to Britain in disgrace because he wanted to marry a girl from a lower class. Although the patient felt bitter about his father's authority and the subsequent marriage of the girl, it was clear that he was also lonely and homesick. At first the social worker avoided discussion about this man's difference with his doctor or about his father's right to exert authority over him, as this would have questioned his loyalties and might have widened the rift with the family with whom he still felt strongly identified. In the second interview the patient appeared more vivacious; he had returned to work and while speaking about the girl had realised that the memory did not hurt as much as he anticipated. His chest pain had gone. Subsequently, this patient was helped to find a more rewarding job and to widen his leisure interests. The social worker did not concentrate on causes, but assisted him to increase his skills and reduce his isolation. New activity might provide opportunities to improve his social and competitive relationships, for this man had never before had to compete for work or friends.

Family Problems
When family problems were brought to a general practitioner all members of the family might be involved. Nevertheless, the doctor or nurse usually treated patients individually, while the social worker might be in contact simultaneously with several members of the family.

Some families were helped by discussion about their relationships. Once they had come to know the social worker's impartiality it was possible for them to discuss their attitudes towards each other. A smart middle-aged professional woman was referred to the social worker after consulting her doctor because she was sleeping badly. Divorced for many years, she lived with her adult son who was presenting her with a barrier of depressed and silent hostility since he left school the previous year. He neither worked, nor attempted to obtain training or contribute to the home; he did little except mend his motorbike and watch television. In subsequent interviews the son was able to talk about his depression. He gained insight into his mother's bewilderment and loneliness, normally hidden under a veneer of gay social relationships, whose superficiality did nothing to comfort her. Interviews with the mother led her to realise that her seemingly adult son longed for her maternalism; her fear of being let down again caused her to hold her son at arm's length as she did with other people. Once this mother and son started to understand each other better, they were able to take practical measures about the son's work and other social problems. The social worker then gave information about vocational guidance, a topic through which the mother could demonstrate her wish to help and the son could share with her his apprehension about his future. Eventually both mother and son accepted referral for vocational guidance and continued help with their personal difficulties.

Some families are inclined to cast their members into rigid roles of good or bad and may tend to push helpful people into positions which can detract from their helpfulness. This trap is subtle, especially in general practice where patients may 'ask for advice' from their doctor about family problems. Sometimes this is what they want, but 'seeking advice' may be a socially acceptable way of asking for more subtle types of help. Occasionally doctors feel they are expected to 'know' and give definite opinions on the break-up of a marriage, delinquency of a child, or a young person's choice of career. It may be difficult for the general practitioner to see whether the patient really seeks his advice or not, for in some circumstances it seemed that patients expected doctors to be men of immediate social action, as in a medical emergency—in others they wanted him to listen without giving an opinion on the rights or wrongs of a situation. Some families exerted similar pressures on the social worker; their members were unaware of their unrealistic expectations of each other and of the people around them. Occasionally they gained insight through discussions with the social worker and sometimes their attitudes towards each other changed.

Such was the case when a recently widowed mother, ill herself, complained to her doctor about the truancy and uncontrolled behaviour of her younger child whom she saw as her 'trouble' and whom she wanted the social worker to control. The elder son aged 13 she regarded as the sensible one, who seldom went out, had few friends and nursed his mother when she was ill. When in distress the mother would retreat into bed, feeling unwell, telling her children that if they were naughty she would become ill and die suddenly like their father. This mother required information and advice about her financial difficulties, help to obtain employment which enabled her to be home when the children returned from school, and advice on facilities for their care during the long school holidays. Most of all, she needed to discuss her own grief, her sexual deprivation, her resentment at being left alive to carry the burden of her family after a marriage in which her husband had cossetted and protected her. She confided that she wanted to re-marry but felt apprehensive lest her friends and children should disapprove.

During these visits the social worker did not accede to this woman's demands that her young son's behaviour be criticised by someone from the practice. By demonstrating her impartiality and providing regular opportunities for the children to size her up, she gradually gained the trust of the children as well as the mother.

Eventually, both children came to see the social worker of their own accord. The elder son came first in order to discuss his future career. He sobbed to the social worker about the death of his father and his fear that his mother might die. The younger boy followed a few weeks later after a scene with his family. He was tearful and determined and told the receptionist that he wanted an appointment with the social worker because he had left home and needed to find somewhere else to live. The skill of the receptionist in helping unhappy children came into play, for she realised that this child was desperate enough to run away. She persuaded him to stay in the building until the social worker was free. He said that he was going away because everybody at home and at school expected him to be bad. Gradually, the mother became aware that her boys also grieved about the death of her husband. 'Good' and 'bad' child reacted differently, but both needed help, as she did herself. When the role of scapegoat was lifted from the younger child all the family could view referral to a Children's Department as a helpful step and not a punishment. The mother hoped the child care officer would assist her to cope more easily with her children, her own loneliness and her work and financial difficulties. The older son saw the child care officer as an adult who would share his anxiety about his mother's health and advise on his future, while the younger boy viewed this referral as a safe avenue of escape should things at home become too much for him; it was interesting that the ability of the Children's Department to accept children into care was reassuring to this little boy.

Divided Loyalties
Pressures from family difficulties were felt by all members of the practice team. Divided loyalties had to be avoided. This was attempted by discussing the interactions within the family and clarifying the purpose of help, the methods to be used, by whom, with whom and when. Feelings ran high, especially where marital conflict affected the health of a young child. The doctors were often summoned to one child aged 3 whose asthma seemed a barometer of the way her affections were used as a weapon in her parents' marriage. Each parent engaged a solicitor, and constant demands were made on the social worker and the doctors to take sides in their court action. To give effective help, the social worker and her colleagues had to stay outside this vicious circle, accept the resentment of both partners and remain willing to help with the total situation when the couple were ready to compromise. Eventually they accepted a referral outside the practice

for help with their marital problems and reached a decision to separate and apply for a divorce. The little girl's health improved dramatically when her parents separated. It was clear that she received more attention from both parents, and especially her father, after separation, as the time of access permitted by the court was spent exclusively with her. This couple illustrate a situation where the general practice may not always be the best place for continuing help to be given, for both partners wished to retain the esteem of their general practitioner on whose care they might depend in the future. Therefore some couples did not wish their doctor to know too much about their less attractive marital struggles.

Individual Needs
The needs of particular individuals were given priority in other families despite the extra strain on the rest of the family. An exhausted mother was admitted to hospital to recover from the strain of caring for two disabled teenage children, although her absence increased the burden on her husband. Later, both parents were helped to cope with their boys who exploited their mother's indulgence and were stifled by her anxious fussing. Ultimately the whole family needed help; alleviating the difficulties of one did not resolve the problems of the others. They were referred to a family casework agency where they gained some perception of the destructive inter-relationships within the family. These insights helped them to change their attitudes towards each other. Husband and wife had been sabotaging each other's efforts to exercise discipline over their adolescent children. Undue attention given to their sons' disabilities had inhibited their healthy emotional growth towards adult work and sex roles.

Separated Families
Problems were also brought to the practice by patients whose families had split. Often these solitary and unhappy people described a rift in their marriage or with their children. Sometimes they were haunted by self-recriminations. Their longing for unlikely solutions was dealt with sympathetically, but the social worker did not encourage such patients to reach for unattainable goals; this could only increase their depression and experience of failure. Sometimes discussion enabled patients to realise that they were not feeling as hurt now as they had previously. They might realise too that they had so idealised the past that they were neglecting opportunities in the present. While trying to understand what past events had meant, the social worker tried to help those

clients to contemplate present reality and the future, such as finding more comfortable accommodation, a more satisfying job or taking up new leisure interests. More frequently than expected, the increased confidence and equilibrium these patients gained from such changes enabled them to repair damaged relationships. For example, a young woman who had left her husband and child became more confident after finding better accommodation and work and initiated constructive conversations with her husband about their future, in contrast to the hysterical outbursts engendered by previous meetings. A middle-aged woman, less depressed after she moved and made new friends, renewed contact with her only daughter after years of bitter silence.

Crisis Problems

Many crises were referred to the social worker, some of a transitory nature, others necessitating long-term adaptations. Sometimes these were predictable, as in retirement or on the marriage of a child, at other times they were unpredictable, like sudden bereavement. Generally they involved an experience of loss and separation whether arising from change of employment, rehousing or death. Although quick and adequate social work intervention in a crisis was often important, help could easily become intrusive. The social worker had to see a crisis through the patient's eyes and adapt her methods accordingly.

Sometimes the doctor had the unpleasant duty of precipitating a crisis, perhaps by refusing certificates to stay off work or advising a change of job. A middle-aged arthritic widower was told he was not fit to return to the job he had enjoyed for years and where he had many friends. The social worker first made sure that this patient understood what his doctor had told him since the shock of bad news often prevented patients from taking in what followed. Although his doctor told him a more suitable job would help him, this man assumed he would never work again and would become progressively worse. Already he planned to move in with relations whose children got on his nerves. The second task was to prevent the patient from taking panic action. The social worker suggested that he withdrew the notice to his landlady, which he did. The Disablement Resettlement Officer helped this man to find other work, where he made new friends and felt less exhausted. Once past the initial shock, he showed relief at having faced a crisis he had dreaded for years.

Outside events like consequences of the Borough council's housing programme could result in personal crises and necessitate major readjustments. Solutions which appear obvious to observers may not be easy for patients affected by changes in their living conditions, and outside pressures could make such situations intractable. A disabled housebound widow of 83 provides a typical example. She was the last tenant in the house she had occupied for over forty years, and which had been recently bought by the Borough for reconversion. For years, her neighbours, the other tenants and the Borough domiciliary staff had cared for her—now these friends were rehoused in distant parts of the Borough. She was offered a place in a Home on the other side of London, as there were no vacancies locally. Small wonder this old lady was depressed and mistrusted the local authority social workers because she assumed their vested interest in her move. The Housing Department pressed for action, as they were anxious to get on with the conversion of the house. This old lady now turned to her general practitioner, a life-line for many years; she welcomed the practice social worker's help. The first task was to reduce official pressures which inhibited the patient's ability to make decisions. The general practitioner proved invaluable, for the Housing Department were less inclined to suspect procrastination from a doctor than from a social worker. The second task was to help the patient distinguish those spheres in which she had no choice from those in which she had. Several interviews were needed to enable her to see she had to move from the flat. She expressed her poignant memories by taking the social worker into each room, showing her photographs, and the bed in which the people nearest to her had died. Only then could she decide between the alternative of moving into an old people's Home or into a sheltered housing scheme.

To make a decision, this patient, like anybody else, needed information. As she assumed that a modern old persons' Home was 'like the workhouse', descriptions were inadequate and she was taken by the social worker to visit the Home. When she saw its cosy atmosphere and modern facilities, she realised she would be able to enjoy the garden and have a fuller life there than in her own small rooms. Having made her decision, this old lady took charge of disposing of her furniture and sorting out her belongings.

Patients like these were faced with a decision between two un-welcome alternatives. They needed help to identify their choices and weigh up the pros and cons. The social worker had to take different types of action at different times; help them face reality when shock had confused them, listen with sympathy to the repercussions of this shock, be informative and truthful about the choices open and to take prompt action to help implement the decision they made. Finally, she had to stay in touch for a while to see whether the decision was appropriate. If not, the social worker, with the patient, would try to find a better solution.

Terminal Illness and Death

Problems arising from terminal illness and the repercussions of bereavement inevitably occur in general practice. Sometimes these were in the forefront of a request for help, at other times discussions of previous bereavements or a patient's own fear of death were brought up in other contexts. It came as a surprise to the social worker that so many people of all ages should wish to discuss some aspect of death or dying.

The general practitioner decided when and how a patient should be told the implications of his illness. In general, he was not told specifically, for often it seemed he did not wish to know. The social worker learned about the complexities which face general practitioners in terminal illnesses nursed at home, and realised that popular ideas about whether patients ought to be told were facile. The practice team cared about these problems. Nobody considered they had the answers, but all did their best in each situation.

In terminal illnesses the social worker had to be very careful to respond sensitively to patients' and families' needs and not to intrude beyond this. Some clients required the prompt provision of aids and practical services only, as family and friends helped the patient and comforted each other. For many families, 'keeping busy' counteracted the pain of helplessness, at least temporarily. Some people needed the close involvement of the social worker. Frequently a double bluff existed in which patient and family 'knew' the situation, but hid the truth from each other and themselves. Such families sometimes used the social worker to share their feelings with each other, occasionally without mention of the facts they could not voice. Others wished her to be easily accessible and to respect their own ways of coping with a crisis they could hardly bear. This familiar situation arose with a middle-aged man who was nursing his wife through the painful last stages of a terminal illness. He maintained a cheerful attitude to the outside world for he was determined that his wife should not suspect her diagnosis. This man told the social worker that he felt at the end of his tether; he needed someone with whom he could cry in privacy and voice his despair when he wished, without endangering his pride or his determination to remain calm in front of his wife. Perhaps men have few places where they can give vent to their tender feelings. The social worker had the impression that the wife realised her prognosis, but could not admit this either to herself or to her husband. So, for the first time perhaps, this couple who had previously had a close and happy relationship were not communicating their true feelings to each other. With this and other couples it seemed that the tragic last gift of the dying patient to the partner could be collusion in this double bluff to spare both the acute pain of the impending separation.

Casework help during terminal illness can alleviate anxiety in the patient and in the caring relative. The patient may worry about causing trouble, while relations may be concerned about their reactions to the sick—irritability with their demands, revulsion over incontinence or shock at changed appearance and personality. If unexpressed, these pent-up feelings can contribute towards prolonged idealisation of the dead and guilt in the surviving relative, who needs time before he can bring himself to reveal the memories which worry him.

Bereavement

A social worker in general practice can also be of help when bereavement occurs. The response of the practice team to bereavement made a deep impression on the social worker; the doctors immediately visited the bereaved family of any patient they knew. Sometimes the general practitioner was not informed straightaway of a patient's death in hospital. They minded about such failure in communication which they would take up with the hospital, for relatives often assumed that the general practitioner had been informed and told the social worker that they were hurt by his apparent lack of concern.

The attitude of people at the time of death was often vividly remembered for years afterwards. One widow said,

'When my husband died, Doctor G. came to see me in the middle of the night *in his slippers* although he knew he could do nothing.'

In fact, it was obvious that Doctor G. had done a great deal to help this woman. Bereaved people were nervous of their vulnerability and the social worker was asked by some to ensure a sympathetic response by explaining their situation to officials, like those in the Department of Health and Social Security.

The general practitioner might also assist bereaved people during the acute stages of grief by prescribing psychotrophic drugs for a short time. The social worker regarded these drugs as a powerful aid in such situations: a grieving person could at least feel physically better after an uninterrupted night's sleep, even if he awoke only to a fresh realisation of his loss.

Bereaved patients commonly needed joint help from the general practitioner and social worker with the aftermath of physical and emotional exhaustion. Sometimes they were unsure of their right to become patients themselves. Furthermore, they may have coped by mustering reserves of strength which may have given a misleading impression to those around them. One old lady, for example, felt ill and exhausted after she had nursed her husband through a long illness. Family and friends saw her as 'a wonderful woman who always managed by herself'. On bereavement, she told the social worker of her loneliness and her fear of being a burden to her children and grandchildren. The social worker's hint that if she rejected her family's offer of help they might worry about her, enabled her to accept the care that she needed.

The social worker was sometimes asked to help first with the funeral arrangements, with applications for social security benefit or with negotiating new tenancy agreements. Sometimes the practical repercussions of bereavement were considerable; a reduced income or the need to move happened when patients were least able to cope. Direct discussion of their grief was commonly sought when the flurry of activity had abated after the funeral, when they were left to realise the extent of their loss, and people supposed they 'were getting over it'. Patients who had brief contacts with the social worker at the time of death sometimes returned to her later for more extensive help. Other patients sought discussion of their grief and loss from the very beginning and required frequent contact with the social worker during the early months of their bereavement. Yet others primarily needed affection and care from their relatives and sometimes from their general practitioner whom they had known all their lives. For example, two teenagers were taken into their aunt's family when their remaining parent died. The social worker helped the aunt with her own grief and with practical and legal matters which enabled her to give support and comfort to her niece and nephew. The general practitioner was the key person in the situation, for one of these youngsters developed symptoms similar to those preceding the coronary heart attack which had killed his mother.

The kind of relationship the client had had with the deceased

I

sometimes needed to be understood in order to assist with the problems of bereavement. For example, a capable middle-aged, recently widowed woman, who had always run the family's affairs, for the first time in her life had only herself to care about. This was a new experience and she needed help to develop her own potentials. Another patient, however, had lost a relative on whom she had always been dependent; she appeared immobilised in her bereavement because she could not live independently and had no relatives to lean on. The social worker encouraged this patient to depend on her for a time, to get a job and enjoy her spare time. To this woman, making an appointment with a prospective employer, travelling on a strange bus route and facing new work colleagues, presented hurdles which she had never before taken alone. She needed encouragement when she succeeded and reassurance when she failed. The social worker could have told the patient what to do or done it with her, but this would not have increased her self-confidence and would have encouraged an aimless dependent relationship with the social worker.

Unexpected bereavement, arising from death from violent causes, or sudden death from a heart attack produced some of the most difficult situations. The period of disbelief and numbness often caused these patients to cling to helping people like the social worker, whom they needed to see frequently during the early weeks of their bereavement.

Accumulated Stress and Trigger Events
Pent-up anxiety triggered off by another event, sometimes long after the original crisis, was often expressed by patients referred to the social worker. Sometimes these were patients she had met before, including those whose shock after bereavement lasted long. The reality of the death of an absent person may not be felt until long after the event. Immigrant patients had this experience. The parents of a Nigerian teacher were killed in a revolution but the routine of this woman remained unchanged, and although she knew the facts of her situation, she could not realise its implications. Much of her career in this country had been based on anticipating a return to her own land; she had sought education in order to better teach her own people. Her parents were an intrinsic part of her feeling of home. When the long summer vacation came this teacher realised that she had no parents to return to; this time she could not avoid her pent-up grief.

Many such situations happen in more familiar circumstances. Road accidents, death from coronary heart attack, or from suicide are sudden events too painful to be absorbed immediately. Parents whose only son died suddenly while abroad on holiday secretly half-expected his return. Deprived of the sight of the body of their son and with no funeral to attend, the reality of his death partly remained a bad dream to these parents. They regularly awoke in the night, sure, they had heard his key in the door and his footsteps in the passage. Another bereavement triggered their pent-up grief into expression.

Recollections of loss also occurred at anniversaries or at times of reunion like Christmas. Patients the social worker had known contacted her on such occasions, especially on the first anniversary of bereavement. It helped them to know that somebody was in tune with the causes of their distress.

Other patients were referred because the general practitioner felt their distress was inappropriate to the reasons they gave. One woman reacted desperately against the general practitioner's suggestion of a recuperative holiday. Later she told the social worker that the only time she had ever been on holiday was also at the suggestion of a general practitioner, when her mentally ill husband had killed himself while she was away. This patient welcomed an opportunity to discuss the problem she had kept to herself for many years.

The strength of feelings expressed to the social worker could indicate the amount of energy previously expended in repressing them. Such patients would sometimes experience relief quickly, looking brighter and younger after an opportunity to 'get things off their chest', saying, 'Oh, I feel better now', as though some weight had been removed. The social worker treated these reactions with caution, for once some patients began to express their feelings, they might want to tell everything at once lest the opportunity be lost. Such an outpouring was not necessarily cathartic, as people can feel frightened after they have revealed to a stranger at a first meeting too many painful events and feelings not voiced before. It was important to give such patients an opportunity to come frequently at the point when they needed help most—if necessary, several times a week.

Sometimes fear of past events came near to panic. One patient, whose only daughter had committed suicide three years earlier

'felt like a volcano—I long to let it go, but I feel I would never stop crying and be unable to carry on at home or with my work.'

The social worker had to help these patients maintain their routine and rebuild their emotional defences as well as allow them to experience their distress. Walking such a tightrope involved skill, concentration and patience, for such a patient's progress could fluctuate, and contrasting measures were required from the social worker at different times. Sometimes the general practitioner's help was needed to enable the patient to stay away from work temporarily, at other times the same patient needed strong encouragement to maintain his employment. In such situations the social worker had to give much time and remain accessible, and yet the patient also needed a measure of control, for example limiting the lengths of interviews.

These intensive reactions usually lasted a few weeks only, as such patients generally progressed rapidly. Initial intense distress was followed by calmer interviews in which the more typical rehabilitation after mourning took place. Before engaging in such intensive cathartic work, the social worker had to feel moderately sure of her ability to help a particular patient. The social worker's dependability and nerve were vital; if she took fright at the patient's distress he might take desperate action.

The last straw for other patients came less dramatically. The burden of patients caring for chronically ill or disabled people with apparent devotion frequently became obvious in this way, as did the exasperation of parents with their children. Suddenly the doctor might be asked to send a sick person into hospital or treat the caring relative for vague symptoms like backache or feeling tired. A chronically ill patient would tell the social worker his worry and resentment about being a burden and feeling unwanted and helpless.

Incipient Mental Illness
In some cases the social worker aimed at helping with the 'symptom', realising this represented only the tip of an iceberg of difficulty. Even with more skill, time and resources, the social worker would not have extended her aims with patients whose problems arose from deep-seated, often life-long personality difficulties to which they had their own peculiar adjustment. Such relationships as they had seemed to depend upon their rigid patterns, and trouble could start for them when this was disturbed. Such patients experienced much difficulty in adjusting to change, like finding new accommodation or work, or trusting new people like the social worker.

Staff changes at work, new neighbours or a quarrel with a friend were events which could trigger off insecurity and depression in some patients. Such disturbances set in train suspicious thoughts that the people in their lives were against them and patients brought this kind of paranoia and depression to their doctor in various guises. Sometimes their complaints were incoherent, at other times they suffered from a genuine physical malaise, or they would demonstrate their agitation by making angry demands for an unrealistic solution. Chronically mentally ill patients were sometimes unable to accept referral to outside agencies, they were not ill enough to be admitted to hospital and yet needed easy access to help when panic hit them. An event perceived by them as a crisis might appear insignificant to other people. The social worker considered that when these patients sought help, brief intervention might prevent major crises. The general practice might be the only place to which these patients could turn; the traditional type of casework was not appropriate, nor was group work, as they could disrupt any group or club by being 'difficult'. The social worker learned to be firm and directive in interviews with these patients, for she needed the facts of the present situation and tried to discourage long descriptions of fantasies, unrealistic hopes or anger with people currently seen as 'enemies'. These clients were not relieved by their outpouring of feeling as others were; they might become more frightened and see the social worker as caught up in their chaotic perceptions. By sympathetically stemming their flow of words, focussing firmly on the facts and evolving a realistic plan of action, the trust of some of these patients was gained and it was possible to help them. Unless these limited aims were adopted, months of 'circular' discussion could follow, centred more upon the patient's suspicion of the social worker than on making his present life a little more tolerable for him.

A single woman of 58, living alone, provides an example. Orphaned as an infant, she spent an unhappy childhood in large Homes, and was lonely in the residential employment in which she spent her youth. Eventually she obtained her own room and a factory job in which she had been 'happy' for over thirty years. She said her friendships had always ended in disaster; it seemed that she became suspicious of people's activities and loyalty. The present crisis came when a new manager at work moved her to an easier job on the conveyor belt, which brought new relationships with which she could not cope. She had always been sure that 'everybody' at work was against her but she had previously coped by keeping herself apart. Now this fantasy had become reality, for people complained and her hostility was openly directed towards everybody, especially the manager. She was due to retire in two years' time and receive a pension; long service only had averted a premature dismissal. Gaining this patient's trust was a slow process. Gradually she was able to show the social worker her other side, which longed for appreciation and approval, and she eventually allowed the social worker to ask the firm's personnel officer to help. As a result she was placed under an older manager, given a job in which she could take pride and where it was again unnecessary for her to converse with anybody.

The social worker knew that once such a patient designated people as 'bad', feelings could not easily be reversed. Yet, the confidence gained from resolving her work problems enabled this patient to accept help in widening her social interests, since the social worker foresaw that this woman could become sadly isolated after her retirement.

Problems in Community Relationship

Changes in the community in which they lived produced difficulties for some patients. An attempt to divert these patients' anxieties seemed on occasions the best way to help. Elderly people who had lived in a district for many years did not happily accept the multi-occupation of houses previously owner-occupied, especially if new tenants were different in age, nationality or colour. These attitudes were not attributable entirely to prejudice, but contained bewilderment at the passing of familiar patterns and their replacement by strange people and customs. The social worker tried to find ways in which these patients could extend their interest outside their homes, for she could not turn back the clock, which is what they were seeking.

Flat-dwellers presented problems arising from lack of relationships within a community, for the close proximity of people in blocks of flats could create relationship barriers which increased the isolation of those tenants who were not employed—housebound mothers with young children or the elderly, living alone. From the social worker they required information about community activities in their area, and help to participate in these.

Similarly, some children who did not easily make friends with their peers had considerable problems in fitting in to the large comprehensive schools. Sometimes the practice became involved in negotiating a change of school for such children.

Unsuccessful Short-Term Help

When the social worker was clear that she was not helping a patient, she discontinued contact, while assuring the patient that she and the practice team were available if he wished. A middle-aged widow and her 80-year-old deaf aunt lived a dreary, depressed and hostile existence.

The younger woman enjoyed her job where she had friends, but dreaded her approaching retirement. The elderly aunt remained shut away in her deafness. Despite nine interviews between the practice social worker and both patients, individually and together, the situation remained unchanged. The help of a local-authority Welfare Department worker was also enlisted in attempts to offer the deaf woman aids or leisure activities. Although both patients asserted that such activities would help, there was always some reason why their participation was not possible. It was clear that both these women were embedded in their routines; although they were monotonous and depressing, they did not wish to take any steps to change the patterns.

Summary
Short-term help in which the social worker concentrated on assisting patients with their current situation was the social work method most frequently used in this project.

It was appropriate when families involved their general practitioner in their social problems, for members of some families who would agree to meet a social worker in their general practice would not go to a social work agency until they had tested a social worker's help.

Crisis situations, arising from physical or mental illness or bereavement often responded to a social worker's help when it was quickly available and associated with the continuing care patients received from their doctor. Pathological grief was especially susceptible to help in this context, for medical expertise could be quickly enlisted if grief had severe repercussions on health.

Finally, chronically mentally ill patients, their families and patients with 'difficult' personalities often regarded their general practitioner and the social worker as life-lines when in trouble. Sometimes they had rejected or been rejected by other sources of help. Brief social intervention helped these patients to keep going and perhaps averted more serious difficulty.

LONG-TERM HELP

Long-term help consisted of more than twelve interviews over longer than three months and was given in 148 episodes. Some patients in similar situations to those already described needed and received long-term help. In most of these cases, however, the nature of the contacts differed because of the types of problem the patients faced or because of the personality or expectation of the patients themselves. Some patients received help over a long period because they returned to the social worker three or more times. These clients we have called 'high users'. A patient may have used short-term help on one occasion, or long-term help on others and, at yet other times, assessment and clarification may have been all that was required. Only seventy-one patients came into this 'high user' category, but as they took up proportionately twice as much social work time as any other group of patients, we shall describe them separately at the end of the chapter.

Some patients needed help from their general practitioner for many illnesses and disabilities affecting them and their families. These patients also sought help from a social worker in close touch with their doctor. For example, in one family the wife had severe bronchitis, her husband was chronically mentally ill, their unmarried daughter was pregnant and their son in prison. Progressively ill patients also clung to the general practice and sometimes required a lengthy contact with the social worker before they could accept a social worker outside the practice.

Repercussions of a long and painful illness sometimes required the social worker to stay in touch with a family through this experience without having clear aims, but helping, in the ways the patients wanted, with each difficulty as it arose. As a typical example, and one which illustrates the ups and downs of such work, we want to describe the longest case in the project. The social worker remained in contact with this family for three and a half years and often felt at a loss to know what to do. While in hospital the husband had been told the diagnosis and prognosis of his terminal illness. This illness had coincided with the birth of this couple's only child, who had turned out to be physically disabled. After his self-discharge home this man refused help from everybody except his general practitioner. When a local authority social worker called with a back-rest, he threw it out of the door and threatened to throw out the worker as well. He would not open the door to a nurse or home-help. The social worker was admitted only because she worked with the general practitioner and was personally introduced by him. Though polite to his doctor, the man raged at everybody else, most of all at his wife, who was thin, cowed and frightened, torn between the demands of her husband and her devotion to her disabled baby. Through business failures, this couple had moved from upper-class comfort to their present poverty. As the patient would not allow his wife to clean or move anything in his room, the dust and grime increased and the curtains hung in ribbons.

This man would not accept any other helpers and so the social worker had to persevere, although she often dreaded the visits. The patient was always glad to see her, which made the social worker feel worse about her inability to make any suggestion which stood any chance of being accepted by him. His anger towards her did not worry the social worker unduly, as she could sense the desperation behind it, but she was worried by the hatred he showed towards his wife. He bitterly resented the attention his wife gave to the baby, and she was being gradually worn down by the impossible demands being made on her. The patient did not allow his wife to speak to the social worker on her visits to the family. Occasionally the wife would seek out the social worker at the practice, and make her promise never to tell her husband about the visit. During the first months the patient made angry demands on the social worker to write to authorities in various parts of the world to find a cure for his illness. He made it plain in each interview that he considered she was no good, but then would confirm the date and time of her next visit.

As his anger subsided, he started to tell the social worker what he feared might be the repercussions of his illness; never had she been so glad to be 'non-medical', for she could not be expected either to confirm or deny his fears. It was often difficult to know what to say, and frequently she said nothing. The patient often gripped her hand during these visits and then would lie holding her hand without speaking. One afternoon, because she had less courage to listen than he had to talk, she started to 'reassure' him, to be met with an outburst of anger which made her realise that she had let him down. During later months, the wife would come in and sit on the bed putting the baby beside him. Sometimes he shouted at his wife, while gently stroking the baby.

His illness lasted eighteen months from the time he left hospital. He never allowed his room to be cleaned, nor did he ever use a back-rest. In the last few weeks he was admitted to hospital and the social worker took the wife and baby in her car to see him daily, waiting outside during their visit. The ward sister described these visits as peaceful, with the baby on the bed admired by everyone in the ward.

At the funeral, there was just the wife, the baby and the social worker. Despite being sworn at, insulted and ignored, the neighbours collected for a wreath which they sent as from the baby.

In the following weeks the social worker and the general practitioner became very worried about the physical and emotional debility of the wife who, apart from caring for the baby, did little except sit in her husband's room which was exactly as he had left it. She did not wish to go into a hospital or nursing home with the baby, nor was she willing to see a specialist. At the time when it seemed that some action like this might have to be taken, she moved a few of her husband's possessions to the other side of the room; she had bought a new curtain and asked the social worker to help her clean the window beside her husband's bed. Taking down the old curtain and cleaning the window together seemed to be 'letting in the light'. Slowly, she started to care for herself; previously she had spent most of her money on food and comfort for her husband and child. The first 'luxury' she allowed herself was a pair of warm boots which she and the social worker bought out of the practice patients' fund. Gradually more people came into her life. She made a good relationship with the local health visitor and she began to discuss matters with the hospital social worker at the pediatric clinic which she attended with the baby. She allowed the practice volunteer and her friends to clean and decorate her flat and enjoyed their lively company. She tried and rejected a therapeutic group for young mothers. Throughout this time she also wished to remain in touch with the practice social worker, probably because sharing the experience of her husband's long illness and death had created a special bond. The social worker realised this and stayed in touch, but she also encouraged this patient to make new friendships with her neighbours, other social workers and with people she met at the various clinics she now attended. There were many setbacks, for problems arose about the baby who, as a toddler, developed temper tantrums. To the social worker, however, these outbursts seemed healthier than the passive, withdrawn infant she had known before. In the two years following her husband's death the social worker watched a transformation in this woman, from being thin, haggard and prematurely aged, to the bright, good-looking young woman she turned out to be. Eventually, when the project ended she was transferred to the hospital social worker whom she already knew.

With other patients limited intelligence affected the pace of progress and so necessitated a long contact. Helping a warm-hearted woman who had no relatives and who was epileptic, deaf and mentally retarded to find new accommodation took months, especially as she had a collection of adored pets to take with her. Eventually this patient moved in with a housebound patient who was finding it hard to cope with daily domestic chores. This arrangement worked well for them both, as their needs were complementary and luckily they enjoyed each other's company. Such patients required practical help, information and advice, combined wih sympathy and understanding. Services and information had to be offered at the right time, changes in physical and mental health made different types of service necessary over a long period. Some of these patients did not wish to be referred to social workers outside the practice; sometimes they accepted referral when they realised that the local authority social worker was also in touch with their general practitioner. Often it helped these families to meet local authority social workers in the practice.

Patients whose medical diagnosis was uncertain or who awaited further medical treatment were among those given extended help. The waiting period preceding treatment could be painful and full of fear. Supporting the patient through this time was part of the general practitioner's work and the social worker was asked to help with the many social and psychological problems during this uncertain period. Occasionally the medico-social diagnosis was modified as a result of the social investigation. A professional woman in her twenties vented her bitterness on the general practitioner and the social worker after her face had been badly cut in a car accident. At first this was attributed to shock; while in hospital this patient feared she might be blind, as her eyes were bandaged and nobody had told her the nature of her injuries. The sight of her scars appalled her and it was hard to wait the months before her need for plastic surgery could be assessed. Gradually it became obvious that this tragic situation was not the only burden this young woman carried. She described to the social worker her deep unhappiness before the accident, her wish to die and her resentment that the crash had disfigured but not killed her. The scars on her face faded; surgery was unnecessary, but she allowed the general practitioner to refer her to a psychiatrist for treatment of her depression, which may have been responsible for her accident.

Occasionally patients for whom the social worker had planned only brief support while they awaited an appointment with a psychiatrist started to make definite progress. When this happened the case was discussed with the general practitioner and often with the psychiatrist. Sometimes after an assessment, the psychiatrist suggested the social worker should continue to treat the patient but consult him if she thought this necessary. A single man, professionally qualified, in his mid-twenties came as a new patient to the practice to complain of his depression and to describe his fear of becoming addicted to drink and hard drugs. His tramp-like appearance belied his upper-class background; his inarticulate and confused speech was incongruous with the excellent degree he had recently obtained. The social worker and the doctors considered this man should be seen by a psychiatrist for an assessment. He had to wait several weeks for an appointment and during this period visited the social worker regularly because he feared he might commit suicide and needed some personal contact which might reduce the risk of him taking such action. To everybody's surprise, not least the social worker's, discussion of his situation and support, together with practical help over obtaining more suitable employment produced definite signs of improvement. His psychiatric appointment was held in abeyance, but the psychiatrist offered to advise the social worker. After three months the patient had transformed his appearance, was no longer taking drugs and was drinking normally on social occasions. He had obtained an academic job for himself near home and was planning to rejoin his family.

A few people were given long-term help because they and the social worker liked each other, and the social worker was interested in helping them. In her previous employment in a family casework agency the social worker had worked with long-term multi-problem family situations and wanted to continue this work with a few families. A widow with two adolescent children was a typical example. In her first interviews with the social worker she shared intimate details of severe war-time experiences which she had not voiced to anybody before. Sometimes people find it easy to talk to each other for no obvious reason, except that they feel they speak the same language. Such a relationship developed between the mother, her two children and the social worker who knew that she could be of help to them and thought that it might take another worker a couple of years to arrive at a similar position of mutual trust and confidence.

Extended contact was retained with other families because the social worker and the practice team felt so strongly about their plight that they wished to press for change in their situations. The complicated restrictions placed on earnings of widowed mothers, and the anomalies in financial assessments for their contribution towards day-nursery fees were familiar problems to the general practice team. Such situations were always taken up with the authorities if it seemed that the patient was not receiving all the help to which she was entitled. The 'wages stop'[1] and the restrictions placed on the use of recuperative holidays were also subjects often under discussion. Acute housing problems of ill or disabled people, which required extended negotiations between the practice, the local authority and private housing trusts aroused possibly the strongest feeling within the practice team. Appeals to local councillors and MPs were often of no avail; but the social worker and the doctors felt they had to continue their efforts. One elderly couple lived in two rooms on the fourth floor of an old house, with a leaky roof and rotten floorboards. Their water tap was down one flight of stairs and the lavatory and coal in the basement. The man was in constant pain from arthritis and his wife had fainting attacks. They had been on the local authority housing list for over twenty years, but because they were not overcrowded they had little prospect of being rehoused. With convenient accommodation they could have lived active and useful lives, but as it was, even the journey to and from their front door was an exhausting experience. The husband had lived and worked in the Borough all his life, except for army service during both world wars. When the project ended this couple were still in their dilapidated rooms, the husband becoming more withdrawn into the loneliness of his constant arthritic pain.

The 'High Users'

As already said, a small group of patients, 71 out of 770 people who had personal contact with the social worker, returned to the social worker for three or more episodes of varying lengths. These patients represented the hard core of social problems brought to this practice. In four-fifths of the cases their social problems were connected with physical or mental illness, often severe, progressive or terminal. For

---

[1] The 'wage stop' limits the amount of supplementary benefit a person can receive to the amount he would have earned in full-time work, with certain allowances for working expenses (*Supplementary Benefits Handbook,* para. 68).

example, sixteen patients were bedridden or housebound or seldom got out of doors. They and other physically ill 'high users' suffered from conditions like chronic bronchitis, arthritis, severe heart troubles, multiple sclerosis or muscular dystrophy. Two patients had epilepsy which could not be controlled by drugs, there was a spastic girl, and a few elderly people, now very frail and weak. Five patients had young children who were blind, congenitally malformed or mentally retarded. Ten patients had schizophrenia themselves or in the immediate family, while four families included a person suffering from a severe phobia.

It is understandable that these patients sought social help which was closely integrated with medical care and near to their homes. For all of them, the general practice was the place to which they turned for help, whether this was associated with health, housing, work, family or personal crises. Often other social workers were in touch with these patients, but when crises loomed they returned like homing pigeons to their general practitioner and the social worker who was part of the team. The problems they presented differed from other patients in that twice as many had problems related to work, school or social isolation. Also they more often had financial or housing problems or needed domiciliary services.

With some, the social worker and the practice team could not hope for improvement in the patient's medical or social condition. The aim was to keep things ticking over, for 'progress' often entailed maintaining a status quo or delaying deterioration. Elderly patients who were just managing at home could be seriously affected by a cold spell in the weather, the illness of a home-help, or an electricity cut. Similarly, the tenuous stability of a family containing a mentally or physically ill parent was maintained providing there was no unexpected change or stress. An attack of influenza in the parent who was well could mean a major crisis when the frail structure of the family might collapse. The social worker tried to anticipate some of these crises and where possible took prompt action to ameliorate their effect. Simple practical action was sometimes all that was needed. For example, if a mother had to attend hospital with a sick child, she might be less harrassed if a reliable volunteer met her other children from school.

Some physically ill patients were in pain and needed to tell this to the social worker. Sometimes people who suffered prolonged or acute pain, like the arthritic, felt that neighbours and friends were tired of hearing about their suffering and that their life of pain held a particular loneliness. Other patients were frightened of their illness, like the epileptic, or they might feel it carried some social stigma—as for example, those with skin complaints. Sometimes mothers were guilty about illness in their children or disliked giving them the medical treatment which was necessary—as in the case of children with asthma or eczema.

Some patients needed different services at different times. A chronic bronchitic patient was active and independent for one part of the year but bedridden at other times. Another patient, progressively ill, reached a stage of adaptation but a new symptom, a tremor in his hand, reawakened former fears which had immediate repercussions on his family relationships. Similar fluctuations occurred with mentally ill patients. When the patient was well and the family functioning without strain, the social worker withdrew. Other patients required phased intervention because they were only able to take one step forward at a time. Some appeared weakly motivated for change, because to patients who laboured under severe problems, the devil they knew could be preferable to the risk of any change. For example, a young, severely disabled patient, whose small family circle was adjusted to his disability, needed time to consider whether he was ready to face new relationships in a sheltered workshop. Another older man who lived alone had a severe chest condition which was considerably aggravated by the dusty atmosphere at his place of work. Yet this man preferred illness and pain to giving up his job because this meant the risk of losing friends he had known for over thirty years. Only when a group of volunteers had demonstrated their consistency through two years' visiting did this patient relinquish his job for other activities.

The social worker was in touch with other agencies on behalf of most high user patients. She tried to find ways of linking other social workers with the general practitioner, whose role was so important to these handicapped patients. She was sometimes able to explain the needs of individual patients and to ask for flexible procedures. Finally, especially with housing problems, the social workers and the general practitioners continually acted as advocates for unmet needs of the ill and disabled.

Summary

Long-term and periodic help to 'high user' patients was required with those families or individuals who had many physical and mental handicaps, calling for the constant surveillance of the general practitioner. Often these families wanted help from the practice social worker. Occasionally they would extend their allegiance if they observed a good relationship between their general practitioner and a social worker from the local authority department.

Patients of limited intelligence sometimes seemed to regard the practice team as substitute parents. It was difficult for them to accept any source of help which did not have the open door and informality of the general practice.

Patients awaiting further medical treatment often had many social difficulties too and required help from a social worker who was in close touch with their doctor.

The practice team chose to sustain their effort as advocates for the improvement of harmful conditions—bad housing, for example, which inhibited a patient's social adjustment or damaged his health.

BIBLIOGRAPHY

Note

No references have been included in Chapters 8, 9, and 10, as these concentrate on the actions taken with individual clients. We are aware that the social worker's practice was influenced by an amalgam of theory and examples derived from her training and other sources. We have selected a few of these sources:

BALINT, M. *et al.* (1964), *The Doctor, His Patient and the Illness* (2nd ed.), London, Tavistock.

BOTT, E. (1970), *Family and Social Network* (2nd ed.), London, Tavistock.

CANADA, Dept. of National Health and Welfare, Emergency Health Services Division, Ottawa (1967), *Management of Human Behaviour in Disaster*.

FAMILY DISCUSSION BUREAU (1962), *The Marital Relationships as a Focus for Casework*. Welwyn, Herts., Codicote Press.

FAMILY DISCUSSION BUREAU (1955), *Social Casework with Marital Problems*. London, Tavistock.

GOLDBERG, E. M. (1959), 'The Normal Family : Myth and Reality,' *Social Work*, *16*, (23–8; 54–62).

GOLDBERG, E. M. (1966), *Welfare in the Community*. London, National Institute for Social Work Training.

GORER, G. (1965), *Death, Grief and Mourning*. London, Cresset.

HINTON, J. (1967), *Dying*. Harmondsworth, Penguin.

LAING, R. D. (1971), *The Politics of the Family*. London, Tavistock.

LEWIS, C. S. (1957), *The Problem of Pain*. (1st ed. 1940), London, Fontana.

LEWIS, C. S. (1966), *Grief Observed*. London, Faber. (First published, 1961).

NEWSON, J. and NEWSON, E. (1963), *Infant Care in an Urban Community*. London, Allen & Unwin.

PARKES, C. MURRAY (1964), 'Effects of Bereavement on Physical and Mental Health', *Brit. Med. J.*, *ii*, (274–9).

PARKES, C. MURRAY (1965), 'Bereavement and Mental Illness,' pts. 1 & 2, *Brit. J. Med. Psychol.*, *38*, (1–26).

PARKES, C. MURRAY (1970), 'The First Year of Bereavement: A Longitudinal Study of the Reaction of London Widows to the Death of their Husbands', *Psychiatry*, *33*, (444–67).

SUSSER, M. W. and WATSON, W. (1971), *Sociology in Medicine* (2nd ed.), London, Oxford Univ. Press.

TEBBUTT, KATE (née LEWIS), Lecture notes (unpublished).

RUDDOCK, R. (1969), *Rules and Relationships*. London, Routledge & Kegan Paul.

WOLFF, SULA (1969), *Children Under Stress*. London, Allen Lane, The Penguin Press.

YOUNGHUSBAND, E. (*ed.*) (1966), *New Developments in Casework*. London, Allen & Unwin.

K

11

COLLABORATION WITH OTHER AGENCIES

A genuine 'open door' policy in which the social worker was ready to see all comers with as little delay as possible and to take on emergencies immediately, implied flexibility in methods and aims and a limited, regular caseload. In any case, as already explained, our intention was to limit social work treatment to those who would accept help only within the practice and to people in crisis situations, and to use other social services as widely as possible for the rest. This was done with an eye to the future, as it would not be feasible to attach a full-time social worker to each group practice. Many considerations entered into the decision to refer patients to another agency: was there a resource in the community which could help this particular patient equally well, or better than the practice social worker? Was the patient willing to consult someone else? Was the doctor agreeable to such a plan?

Some patients quite simply needed more time than the practice social worker could give. Others needed specialised help, such as group therapy or help from more than one social worker in complex family situations. Yet other patients needed attendance at day centres or clubs, rather than individual casework. Occasionally adolescent boys required the help of a male social worker, and so on. When patients were 'referred' to another social agency the responsibility for helping them with their social difficulties was passed from the social worker in the practice to a colleague outside. During the four years of the project 381 people were referred to other agencies. The practice team often reminded themselves that 'When we refer a patient we must not kid ourselves that we have done anything.' Introducing one person to another was a beginning, not an end in itself. This applied equally to referrals made within the practice team.

When help from other agencies was enlisted for patients who remained under the care of the practice social worker, these transactions were not called 'referrals', as responsibility for only one aspect of a patient's problem was passed on, and not the whole situation.

These 'agency contacts' will be discussed at the end of the chapter.

Referrals could take place at three different stages of the patient's contact with the practice social worker. In the majority of cases (198 patients) the decision to refer resulted from the initial assessment and was the main method of dealing with the case. The social worker thus did not become involved in a treatment relationship. Secondly, with a considerable number of patients (148) the social worker did become involved in short-term treatment, perhaps during some crisis, and subsequently referred the patient on for more extended help. Bereavement which necessitates an immediate response and short-term help is a situation where additional long-term help may be needed with readjustments, like managing on a reduced income, finding new employment, coping with delayed reactions of grief or its repercussions on children. Thirdly, a small group of twenty-five patients was referred to other agencies as a preventive measure against future need after a period of prolonged help from the practice social worker, which sometimes extended over several episodes. Progressive illness often carries with it the threat of future crises and the patient and his family need to know where to turn at such times. Also the social worker did not know whether a successor would be appointed to the practice at the end of the project; whereas the social work services in the Borough would remain, though their staff might change.

The Agencies
The many teaching and specialist hospitals in and around Camden had large medical social work departments. As these hospitals accepted patients from all parts of the country and also from overseas, their social workers had allegiance to other spheres of work as well as to the local Borough. Despite their wide responsibilities many hospitals were making imaginative efforts to improve their services for the local population. For example, one hospital was providing a geriatric home-visiting team consisting of consultant geriatrician, physio-therapist, hospital social worker and occupational therapist. The general hospital which catered for most of Caversham practice patients, however, had only three medical social workers at the time of the project. They were fully occupied with the problems of the many hundreds of rapidly changing in-patients of the hospital. The psychiatric hospital for the catchment area of the general practice was outside the Borough and, although its social work department was steadily increasing in size during the years of the project, it was seldom

possible to refer out-patients to these psychiatric social workers because of the great distances involved.

The Tavistock Centre provided out-patient psychotherapeutic treatment which was much in demand. In general, this centre tended to accept only patients with a good prognosis, who were reasonably intelligent and articulate. Patients who were accepted received skilled treatment, but often after waiting for many months.

The local authority personal social services (Children's, Health and Welfare) were accommodated together in a large building situated centrally in the Borough, but away from the shopping districts frequented by most practice patients. For many patients this journey presented no problems, but for some elderly, disabled or anxious patients it was difficult and occasionally impossible to manage. The formality of the large building was another deterrent to patients who feared taking an automatic lift and who became confused trying to find the correctly numbered room in a long corridor. The local authority social workers were quite willing to visit patients in their own homes, but this did not *always* solve the problem of their accessibility in times of crisis.

The two geriatric health visitors who covered most of the practice area worked from an infant welfare clinic close to the main shopping street and very near to the practice. Elderly people found these workers easy to contact and liked the cosy atmosphere of the small welfare clinic.

The Borough had an enterprising and thriving Council of Social Service which was situated near the local authority central offices. This building was unpretentious, in a main street and had many notices over the door, including one for the Citizens' Advice Bureau. Although it was as far away as the local authority departments and also had an automatic lift, patients seemed to find the Council of Social Service less 'official' to visit than the local authority departments. The three trained caseworkers who comprised the casework section of the council were often asked to help Caversham patients. Their policy could in some respects be more flexible than that of statutory departments; they were able to take on people who only worked in the area and those who lived just outside the Borough in adjoining Islington, near to the Council of Social Service office in King's Cross. The most successful period of co-operation occurred during a year when the Camden Council of Social Service used a small consulting room over a café in the busy shopping street near to the general practice. Other departments of the Camden Council of Social Service filled gaps in provisions, such as their bureau for the part-time employment of retired people, and their volunteer bureau which acted as a clearing-house for volunteers and was run by a full-time organiser. They also provided four Citizens' Advice Bureaux in the Borough, one of which was near the practice and was freely used by patients and practice staff.

The housing welfare officer, although without a local office, was easy to introduce to patients for she was a familiar face in the area. Although only those living in local authority accommodation were officially eligible for her help, the practice social worker often consulted her on other housing matters. People knew who she was, just as they knew the district nurse, because they were often seen about.

The General Practitioners and the Social Services

At the start of the project, the general practice team felt there were a lot of social workers in the area, but that they did not know them personally nor what they did. The practice social worker soon discovered that one of her important tasks was to build bridges between members of the practice team and other providers of help for patients.

It was easier to achieve liaison between the doctors and the social workers in the community if they had met at least once. The introduction of the local geriatric visitors and the caseworkers of the Camden Council of Social Service was easily accomplished; but the many social workers in the statutory departments were more difficult to identify as persons. Most of the local authority departments divided their staff into teams for different areas of the Borough. Since the practice extended to several areas, at least twenty social workers were concerned with the practice population. In time most of these social workers visited the practice and came to know the staff. The case discussions over lunch at the Caversham Centre provided opportunities for social workers to meet the practice team, to co-ordinate their aims and to explore and discuss difficult cases. Sometimes social workers from different settings—in the local authority, in voluntary organisations or in hospitals—met each other for the first time at the practice; they also met people from other fields concerned with the patient, such as hospital doctors and teachers. In these informal discussions frustration could be brought out into the open—for example, the doctors sometimes became irritated by the need to emphasise one aspect of a problem, say children's needs, in order to refer a family to the Children's Department. Would the Children's Department pay attention to all generations, including the elderly, the doctors wondered. Area boundaries could produce problems, if different members of a split family lived in different parts of the Borough and close liaison within the department was necessary. If members of a family lived in different boroughs co-ordination was needed to decide responsibility for any cost arising. Such considerations were of course important to the administrator who holds the purse strings on behalf of the ratepayers, but to a general practitioner the delays involved can be irritating and hard to understand.

Some social workers 'dropped in' to the practice when they were in the area. The two local geriatric visitors, some child care and mental welfare officers and also the housing welfare officer developed a friendly and relaxed relationship with the team. The members of the practice readily availed themselves of these opportunities to discuss and, when appropriate, to refer cases. Thus, as time went on more and more patients were referred to other social workers directly by the doctors, but unfortunately we did not keep a record of these changes. Understandably, whenever a doctor wished to refer a patient directly, he would tend to bypass the formal 'intake' procedure of the department and telephone the person he knew. This illustrates the general practitioner's need to deal with persons he can trust, rather than with official organisations. The people with whom they most easily discussed their patients were not necessarily the most senior staff, but those who responded quickly to a request, had good memories, quick access to information, were frank about what was possible and expressed themselves concisely. Sometimes the practice team had never met the person they 'knew'. For example, for years they had telephone conversations with a secretary attached to a hospital geriatric unit and regarded her as a trusted colleague; when she visited the practice she was greeted like an old friend.

Patients' Attitudes Towards Referral

Many patients knew little or nothing about social work. Over half of all clients referred to the practice social worker had apparently never met a social worker before. The ease with which most patients accepted social work help from somebody who was a member of the general practice team did not always indicate their attitude towards social work in general. While they expected and understood a referral by their general practitioner to a hospital specialist, their understanding of a referral to a social worker outside the general practice could never be taken for granted.

Some patients associated social work departments with social stigma, assuming that the local authority social services were primarily for the poor, the social failures or the delinquent. Others feared the power of these departments and saw their functions as authoritative—removing children into care, or putting elderly or mentally ill people 'away' into homes or hospitals. There were also those who were surprised and gratified to learn that material and caring facilities existed which they had a right to use. For example, it was rare for somebody experiencing a marital problem or bereavement to know that help could be obtained for personal or family worries. Most patients expressed a need for 'somebody to talk to', yet their most common fear about going to a social worker outside the practice was that they would not know how to describe their problems. Often such patients had talked easily to the social worker in the practice.

The practice social worker was surprised to meet so many physically handicapped people who had not heard either of the Welfare Department or of the variety of aids available. For example, a wealthy man who had suddenly gone blind was much assisted by the training facilities and aids he received after his referral to the Welfare Department. He had never met the medical social worker during his time as a private patient in hospital; after his discharge he bought expensive equipment which was inferior to that provided by the statutory services. Like other upper-class patients, this man thought that he was ineligible for statutory social services and assumed that because they were free they were bound to be inferior.

In general, the lack of knowledge about social services amongst patients of all ages and social classes was surprising.

Methods of Referral

Apprehensive patients could be helped to accept a referral if the practice social worker (and sometimes their doctor as well) spent time and care on deciding which was the most suitable agency and person to whom to introduce them. This 'pre-referral' assessment and planning was also important for other reasons. A good experience of referral was less likely to be interpreted as a rejection. It was more likely to result in a fruitful relationship between the patient and his new helper, and it might also enable him to seek help at an early stage of any future difficulty. The social worker's assessment had to include an understanding of the patient's problems and a realistic appraisal of the type and extent of help her colleagues in other departments were able to offer, as distinct from what they would like to be able to do. Pressures of work, staff changes, waiting-lists for day or training centres, different types and levels of social work training and also different abilities of individual workers, all affected the service that could be offered to a patient. It was our impression that patients were ready to put up with some disappointments and inconveniences, provided the reasons were explained to them.

The times at which clients could be seen were a recurring difficulty, as social work departments were open only during the day. Many times patients wanted to see a social worker in the evening, and although most social workers gave evening appointments if requested, they often had to see patients in an empty department in which the receptionist had gone off duty and the switchboard had shut down. The need for flexible hours in social work offices was highlighted by the use patients made of the practice social worker during evening surgery. Indeed, it is probable that some patients, especially young employed adults and older men in responsible jobs accepted social work help only because they could come after working hours. This evening work seemed to recruit clients who would not usually be seen in social service agencies, operating on a nine-to-five basis.

The methods of introducing patients to the social workers in other agencies varied according to their needs. Some wanted to make their own appointments, others liked the practice social worker to do this for them. Some patients felt more at ease if the social worker introduced them personally to her colleague. Initial interviews in which both social workers were present were helpful to nervous people or to patients who had come to know the practice social worker especially well. Some of these patients were very uncertain about their ability to describe painful situations to 'strangers'. Usually the practice social worker stayed for the first half of these interviews and withdrew when she saw that the patient was talking easily with her colleague.

Types of Agencies and Problems
Nearly half (44 per cent) of patients seen and sent on to other agencies were referred to the three social service departments of the local authority (Welfare, Children's and Health). Nearly a third (29 per cent) were referred to the small casework department of the Camden Council of Social Service. Within the local authority services the geriatric visitors were most frequently used. The help of hospital social workers was sought infrequently; only twenty-one patients

were referred to them, although they were consulted on sixty-three other occasions.

Patients who needed help with material and environmental difficulties, such as poor housing, financial troubles, difficulties at work or school, or those who required the provision of domiciliary or day-care services, were introduced more often to the statutory social services than were patients with problems in interpersonal relationships. These were referred more frequently to the caseworkers of the Camden Council of Social Service. A related finding is that two-thirds of the patients introduced to the statutory departments had social problems arising from physical or mental illness, whereas illness figured in only 13 per cent of the cases referred to the Camden Council of Social Service. We have said in earlier chapters that illness, environmental and material problems often occurred together; many such patients needed the domiciliary and day-care facilities which only the local authority departments could provide.

Not unexpectedly, since the project occurred before the reorganisation of the local authority personal social services, over a quarter (28 per cent) of the patients who were referred on, required help from more than one social service. This situation arose most often among the elderly who needed aids or adaptations from the Welfare Department, as well as supervisory visits from the geriatric visitors of the Health Department. Although the social workers concerned tried to co-ordinate their efforts, so that only one social worker kept in touch with the patient, this 'sorting' out could delay help.

The hospital social service and the Welfare Department were also often both concerned with the same patient, for the medical social worker's function usually ended on discharge from hospital when the Welfare Department would resume care in certain cases. If the patient was to receive continuing care, both the hospital and the community social workers needed to be informed about his needs. Lack of liaison between hospital and community services was demonstrated when a patient was discharged home from hospital without prior warning either to the general practitioner or to the local social services. Therefore elderly people living alone or young adults in bed-sitting rooms who had few local contacts might arrive home to cold rooms, unaired beds and no food in their larders. The practice staff was very much aware that the reorganisation of the personal social services would not necessarily affect the problems of liaison between hospital and community services. However, the doctors considered that one of the repercussions of the social work project was to alert the hospital social workers to the need to notify the practice before one of their patients was discharged.

Patients who needed to be referred to more than one social agency often had a variety of social problems and had to be especially well prepared. They therefore had more interviews prior to referral than those who were referred to one agency only, and once referred they had twice as many interviews per year as patients who were referred to one agency only.

Follow-up of Referrals
Social workers who accepted referrals were asked to send a note to the general practitioner to say if they had met the patient, whether they thought they could help and what they planned to do. These reports were filed with the medical notes, so that any member of the practice team was able to contact the right social worker, if necessary. However, the social workers provided very few follow-up reports. As we wanted to know something about the longer-term outcome of referrals we drew a sample of approximately 10 per cent from the 517 referrals made. As these 517 referrals involved 381 people, we had to ensure that no patient appeared twice; we also made sure that a proportion of referrals for each project year was included and that referrals to more than one agency were adequately represented. This random selection identified 51 patients, 41 of whom had been referred to one social worker and 10 of whom had been introduced to 24 different social agencies. Thus 65 postal questionnaires were sent to the social workers who had accepted a referral. If the social worker who knew the patient was no longer with the department, we suggested that the questionnaire should be completed from the files by a senior worker.

The social workers were asked the number of interviews they had had with the patient, the length of their contact, the type of help given or attempted and the reasons for ending the contact. Finally we sought the social workers' views on the referral method, for we wondered whether the close relationship of the practice team with some of their patients had created difficulties in establishing contact. We also wanted to know whether social workers preferred referrals from the general practitioners themselves, rather than from an attached social worker.

Although the 65 questionnaires were sent out one year after the project ended, replies were received on all but 3 (Table 11.1). As these three patients had been referred to more than one agency and one of

Table 11.1

RESPONSE TO FOLLOW-UP OF SAMPLE OF REFERRED PATIENTS

Agency response	*Referrals to one agency*	*Referrals to more than one agency*	*Total number of referrals*
Fully completed questionnaires returned	31	12	43
Clients never seen at agency	6	0	6
No records found	4	9	13
No reply from agency	0	3	3
Number of questionnaires sent	41	24	65

these agencies had completed a questionnaire we had, in fact, some information on all cases. In addition to the three non-responses 19 questionnaires were incomplete: no records could be found on 13 patients (although 8 of these were known to have been seen and given help) and no records existed for the remaining 6 people, because they had never got to the agency. Thus, of the 65 questionnaires 43 (66 per cent) were completed. The agencies to whom this sample of patients had been referred are shown in Table 11.2. When we compared the sample with the total number of referrals made, we found that

Table 11.2

AGENCIES TO WHICH SAMPLE PATIENTS WERE REFERRED

Agency	*Referrals to one agency*	*Referrals to more than one agency*	*Total number of referrals*
Health Department			
Geriatric visitors	8	5	13
Mental health department	4	3	7
Family casework section	2	2	4
Welfare Department	2	5	7
Children's Department	2	1	3
Camden Council of Social Service	13	4	17
Hospital Social Workers	1	0	1
Probation and other	9	4	13
Total	41	24	65

the same proportions (44 per cent) were referred to local authority social services. Similar proportions (32 per cent and 29 per cent) of patients were referred to the Camden Council of Social Service, while referrals to medical social workers were under-represented in the sample.

The value of the questionnaires was affected by the large staff turnover in the local authority. Only 10 of the 34 questionnaires returned by the local authority were completed by social workers who had met the patient; and only three local authority social workers had known the patient throughout. On the other hand, all but 3 of the questionnaires received from the Camden Council of Social Service were completed by social workers who had known the patient throughout.

Most of the cases referred to local authority services were said to be 'still open', while the majority of cases referred to the Camden Council of Social Service had been closed. This contrast may be partly explained by the different nature of the problems for which patients had been referred to the two types of agency. The problems connected with physical and mental ill-health, often referred to local authority services, tended to be chronic, and clearly these patients needed long-term help, possibly for the rest of their lives. The difficulties in family relationships for which patients were mainly referred to the Camden Council of Social Service were more acute and over two-thirds of these cases were closed within six months of referral.

The type of help given to patients varied. The local authority services, especially those concerned with the elderly and disabled, provided practical help for a third of their patients, while this applied only to 2 of the 17 patients referred to the Camden Council of Social Service. Work with relatives, friends, neighbours and colleagues was recorded more often by the local authority workers. On the other hand, the caseworkers of the Camden Council of Social Service more often engaged in discussion of personal and relationship problems and gave more advice on practical, financial or social matters.

None of the social workers considered it was hard to pick up somebody else's case and most of them thought it was helpful that another worker was interested in the patient. On four occasions caseworkers felt that possibly the patient had become too attached to the practice social worker and that too many interviews had taken place before referral. In all but a few instances the social workers regarded the case as fairly typical of the sort of problems they normally encountered. Amongst those considered to be atypical were the problems of middle-class clients. For example, the geriatric visitors thought it unusual that a middle-class widow who needed help in her bereavement should be referred, when no practical services were required. It was also thought unusual to have marital problems of the elderly referred as a main concern.

The 'Open Door' and Referrals
The proportion of patients referred to other agencies fell steadily from first to subsequent episodes. Over half (56 per cent) of the patients seen by the practice social worker during their first episode were referred to other social workers, compared with two-fifths (42 per cent) during their second contact and a quarter (26 per cent) of the patients who returned on three or more occasions.

Sometimes patients treated the practice social worker as a 'general practitioner social worker', returning to her to review the situation, much in the way in which they might return to their general practitioner, if they were puzzled about their medical treatment at a hospital. For instance, the patient's contact with a social work department could be disrupted by a change of social worker. Or a change in the nature of their social problems might necessitate review and access to other specialised help. Such situations demonstrated the splintered nature of the social services at the time of the project and the need for a general social worker.

The return of some patients also reflected certain gaps in social service provisions. For example, domiciliary services for acutely ill or chronically disabled people being nursed at home were often inadequate, especially if the patient lived alone, or the caring relative was frail or elderly. The provision of 24-hour care for an elderly ill patient who is living alone and wishes to to die in his own bed is a familiar problem to general practitioners, social workers and other members of the domiciliary team. The continuing problems of the chronically mentally ill and their families also reflected the inadequacies of the social services and perhaps the need for additional types of service. Socially isolated patients sometimes felt unable to use tidily organised day-care facilities. Yet they needed shelter, warmth, food and a background of human interest if damage to their physical health was to be avoided. A serious deficiency in the Borough's mental health service, as in many other local authorities, was the dearth of hostels.

Some patients who had been referred to another agency during their first contact with the practice social worker, were not again referred when they returned for a review of their problem, but were given help by the social worker and the practice team. In some cases the patient's state of health had deteriorated and this meant that they required co-ordinated help from the team. Sometimes a patient had a social problem which was not tackled by the existing social services. Common examples were people with housing problems, who sought a transfer from one type of local authority accommodation to another. Nobody was employed to organise the housing transfer list of the Borough. Thus the initiative was left to a possibly elderly, disabled patient to search the list and approach other tenants about a transfer. In such cases the practice social worker found that most could be achieved by working in co-operation with the housing welfare officer. Other ill-defined situations, which had not reached crisis point and did not fall within the specific scope of any service, were families whose problems did not reach a dramatic climax but whose situation was emotionally enervating, financially stringent and often mono-tonous and lonely. Similarly, people nursing ill relatives at home often were just 'managing', sometimes with increasing exhaustion, especially if they were themselves employed. The general practice social worker was also occasionally used as a channel for complaints about officialdom, and her advice was sought about how patients could obtain co-ordinated action from official departments.

Social Work with other Professionals and Volunteers
In 42 per cent of the cases referred to her the practice social worker retained responsibility for the care of the patient, but sought the help of other agencies on their behalf. As already mentioned, this process was not termed a 'referral' because responsibility was shared and the practice social worker as well as colleagues in other agencies might have personal contact with the patient and his family. In over half these situations help was sought from agencies to whom referrals were not usually made, agencies which are too numerous and varied to describe in detail. These contacts fell into two broad groups, those with a person who was a paid professional and those with people who worked voluntarily.

Mention has just been made of collaboration with the housing welfare officer. Another frequently used contact was the Citizens' Advice Bureau, situated near the practice whose workers supplied information on many subjects and provided access to legal advice at low cost. The practice social worker also experienced a flexible and helpful response from officials at the local offices of the Department of Health and Social Security, who were particularly sensitive to the needs of some mentally ill people.

Collaboration with the education welfare officers was an important feature in the early detection of children who were starting to stay away from school. Sometimes the general practitioner was the first to spot a child's truancy. It is our impression that closer collaboration between general practitioners and education welfare officers could do much to prevent truancy from becoming intractable. The disablement resettlement officer was a reliable source of help with the work problems of patients, not only because of his own specialised knowledge and skills, but also because he acted as a bridge to other officials in the employment exchange. We discovered that the disablement resettlement officer could give help most effectively if he was introduced to patients early in their illness or disability, long before they were ready to start work. Personnel officers and employers also helped to resolve the employment difficulties of individual patients.

There was frequent contact with the organisers of the home-help and good neighbour services on behalf of physically ill or frail patients and occasionally help was sought from hospital occupational therapists and physiotherapists. For example, a child, deeply shocked by the recent death of her mother could cry only during the heat treatment she received for a minor skin complaint; for several weeks, the physiotherapist sat by her, giving sympathy and comfort during her thrice-weekly treatment sessions.

Financial help on a comparatively large scale was rarely needed; the practice social worker sought grants of money exceeding £50 from charitable trusts on only twelve occasions during the four years of the project. However, she often obtained small amounts for Christmas luxuries for the elderly and poorer families, extra comforts for the ill or disabled or for an occasional taxi fare so that a frail relative could visit a patient in hospital. The response from funding organisations was always prompt and generous. For example, a regimental fund not only provided an old, ill, isolated lady with a television set but offered her a pension as well. Another fund installed a telephone in the home of a patient who had a grave heart condition and lived alone. A religious organisation paid a man's fare to the West Indies so that he could see his ill mother and sort out his family problems. An anonymous benefactor paid for a depressed mother and her adolescent daughter to have a holiday and also provided a chairbound patient with painting materials which made a new hobby possible.

Organisers of volunteers were often used by the practice social worker, both, for patients who needed help and also to provide active patients with new interests in life. The appointment of the organiser of the volunteer bureau coincided with the period of the project, and her skill in finding the right person for the right job was in great demand by the practice. Increased familiarity with the Borough revealed the wealth of voluntary effort which existed for a variety of purposes and age-groups.

The enterprise and vitality of young people channelled through Task Force, Community Service Volunteers and various youth groups proved invaluable for many elderly or housebound patients and their families. These young people engaged in a variety of practical tasks which included laying linoleum, redecorating rooms, caring for the pets of patients who were in hospital and visiting and befriending people who were cut off from the outside world. The more difficult the task, the more these youngsters seemed to enjoy finding a solution. Patients had to be carefully selected and prepared for some of their activities, as a dozen young people might arrive in relays to decorate a room, but these isolated clients derived considerable benefit from meeting young people who were spontaneously kind and had an obvious desire to help.

Active retired people who needed to find some worthwhile activity to fill their time were introduced to the organiser of the volunteer bureau. There seemed to be many settings in which a suitable volunteer could fill an important gap; some lonely and bored people found themselves enjoying part-time voluntary work in hospitals, children's homes, prisons, infant welfare centres or assisting with the clerical and administrative work of other organisations. They showed that having a new interest can make life much happier and that shared activity can enable new friendships to develop between shy people who would feel inhibited in a social gathering. Unfortunately volunteers had few opportunities for meeting other people doing different types of voluntary work.

All these volunteer activities also indicated the potential for voluntary effort which remains untapped and which, if organised and encouraged, could do much to help with the many social problems encountered in general practice. Our impression was that there is scope for reliable volunteers to help in the general practice setting, especially with the care of frail elderly people, large families with young children, immigrant patients who feel lost and alone because of language difficulties. We are aware that the integration of volunteers into teams poses difficulties of organisation, and that time has to be found for supervision and supporting volunteer effort (Aves 1970), but we consider that the benefits to all—patients, volunteers and professionals—would in the long run far outweigh any initial teething troubles.

At one time in the project a group of well, socially conscious patients suggested to the social worker that a patients' association be set up. They considered that an organised group of fit, active and interested people could do much to help others who were less fortunate. Unfortunately, due to pressure of time and lack of accommodation this request could not be followed up. The social worker and the practice team deeply regretted this, but considered that if such an association were to realise its full potential somebody in the practice should be available to give his time freely in the beginning.

Other manifestations of mutual aid were the 'self-help' groups; clubs for the divorced and separated, for ex-prisoners, in-patients discharged from psychiatric hospitals, alcoholics, excessive gamblers and drug-addicts. These were important to those patients who gained most help from people who had previously experienced similar problems. The social worker often noticed that the rules such groups imposed on their members were much sterner and more uncompromising than anything they were likely to experience in individual casework. The authority as well as the support engendered in such groups was obviously therapeutic.

Care of the Housebound
An important part of collaboration with other agencies was the care of housebound patients. The heavy dependence upon others by patients who were confined to their homes, and perhaps to their beds, revealed sometimes the dedicated care of relatives, friends and neighbours gathered round into a special 'domiciliary team', or at other times, the inadequacies of the statutory domiciliary services. The reverse also happened; family and neighbourly support might be lacking and the patient would depend wholly on the statutory health and welfare services.

The social worker tried to identify the person whom the patient trusted most and to work in co-operation with these arrangements. For example, many elderly patients regarded their district nurse with affection and confidence, turned to her with their problems and relied on her to organise the other services they needed. The work of the district nurses extended far beyond the job they were required to do; unobtrusively they popped back in the evening or at weekends

L

to see how their patients were. Officially it was nobody's job to empty the bedridden patient's commode; in practice it was often the district nurse, the home-help, the 'good neighbour', the voluntary worker or simply the person next door who made sure that this was done. Contact with the unrecognised, often unacknowledged people who do the important, ordinary daily tasks for housebound patients was an essential part of the practice social worker's job. Some of these patients were kept going by the community around them, who filled the gaps in the evenings, during the night and at weekends when the statutory services were so thinly spread. These *ad hoc* arrangements, though effective with some patients, could not prevent the occasional tragic situation where an elderly or mentally ill person was suddenly discovered seriously ill, alone in a room, seldom visited by anybody and without food, heat or care. These isolated patients were perhaps people who did not generate ready sympathy from those around them.

Summary
An important function of the social worker was to act as a link and co-ordinator between the general practice and a wide variety of statutory and voluntary social agencies.

There was a striking lack of knowledge among patients of all ages and social classes about available social services in the area, but most of the 371 patients referred to other agencies for help accepted this readily, provided that care had been taken in preparing them and in choosing the right source of help.

Nearly half of the patients sent on to other agencies were referred to local authority social services, often for material and environmental difficulties associated with chronic disability. Nearly a third were referred to the caseworkers of the Camden Council of Social Service, mostly with problems in interpersonal relationships. Over a quarter of those referred needed the services of more than one agency.

In two-fifths of the cases the social worker collaborated with many statutory and voluntary services while retaining responsibility for the case. Volunteers made an important contribution to the welfare of patients.

The care of housebound, chronically or terminally ill patients proved to be a neglected field in which collaboration with many different people was essential.

REFERENCE

AVES, G. M. (1969), *The Voluntary Worker in the Social Services*. Report of a Committee, London, Allen & Unwin.

PART IV

CONCLUSIONS

12

SOCIAL WORK IN GENERAL PRACTICE—
CONCLUSIONS AND REFLECTIONS

In the preceding chapters we have described a four-year-long attachment of a social worker to a group general practice in north-west London. We approached this task in three complementary ways: as a process, tracing the learning experience of a multi-disciplinary team; in quantitative terms, categorising client characteristics, problems, and action taken, and relating these variables to each other; lastly we have used case studies to shed light on the social worker's methods. As the emphasis of the project was on the exploration of the role of social work in general practice these methods of analysis were evolved as we went along. All three approaches, even in their comparative crudeness, have proven fruitful in gaining an over-all view and understanding of this many-sided project.

In this group practice which served nine thousand patients, a thousand people were referred to the social worker. Many more were discussed informally without being referred; in addition, the health visitors often dealt with social problems arising in young families and the practice nurse gave support to yet other patients with social and emotional difficulties. As the practice team came to know the local statutory and voluntary services better they referred an increasing number directly to outside social agencies. These facts indicate that general practice is a good pick-up point in the community where psycho-social problems can be spotted, and help initiated.

The Caseload Profile

We have shown that the clients who made up the social worker's caseload had certain characteristic features: there were twice as many women as men, over a third were elderly and two-thirds were either single, widowed, divorced or separated. A third lived alone. This preponderance of women, the elderly, the widowed and divorced has also been observed in other social work caseloads in general practice as well as in local authority Health and Welfare Departments.

We have suggested that the greater psycho-social morbidity among women, their more frequent surgery attendances, their longevity and their 'expressive' roles in the family may have contributed to the high proportion of women among the social work clients. One also wonders whether the 'female' image of social work and the relative lack of interest and knowledge social workers have about the world of work—in contrast to their intense preoccupation with family relationships—contribute to the fact that men seek less help from social workers than women. Men tend to consult their doctors in the late middle years when serious, often chronic illness and the onset of disabilities affect their work capacity and when anxieties about impending retirement come to the fore. Social workers may need to develop more understanding and skills in dealing with the social repercussions of these problems.

It is clear that the problems of the elderly demand attention from social workers, whether in general practice or in local authority services. The needs of frail, old people for a variety of domiciliary services and better material living conditions were demonstrated in this project as in many other surveys and experiments (Townsend and Wedderburn 1965, Harris 1968, Harris 1971). Old people experiencing problems in family and interpersonal relationships and facing painful adjustments after retirement were also in need of casework skills which are often in short supply and used for younger people. There are pointers here in conjunction with other findings (Tunstall 1968, Goldberg et al. 1970) that a redistribution of skills and resources may be indicated within the social services. Many older people encountered in this project were eager for suitable part-time work or some useful voluntary activity. Here is a great field for more sustained community effort on the part of everyone; for casework and domiciliary services, however sensitively given, cannot replace the feeling of belonging and being needed.

One of the interesting findings in this action study was that the occupational distribution of the social worker's clientele reflected that of the Borough and was not unduly weighted towards the semi- and unskilled occupations. It seems that if a social worker is a member of a general practice team people of all social classes find it comparatively easy to use her: the upper classes may consider that she is not identified only with social welfare and the lower classes may discover that she is easily accessible in a familiar environment. However, we found that the nature of the problems presented to the social worker varied between the social classes. Family problems, many of them revealing very disturbed relationships, were more often presented by clients from the professional and managerial classes, while problems related to ill-health, both physical and mental were more concentrated among patients in semi- and unskilled occupations. Interesting questions arise affecting the policies of social service departments. Has the image of social work as a service for social failures and the deprived deterred some people, especially among the middle classes, from seeking help? Will the area offices of the reorganised personal social services become places to which all sections of the community feel able to take their troubles, much as they now use their local general practitioners? Or will some social service departments want to pursue a deliberate policy of positive discrimination in favour of the poorer and more deprived sections of the community?

Range of Problems and Ways of Helping
Two-fifths of the patients who were referred to the social worker presented definite physical complaints to their doctor in their consultation preceding referral and the rest complained either of vague psychosomatic symptoms, had had a psychiatric illness or consulted the doctor about overt social difficulties, without bringing up any other symptoms.

We have shown that apart from requesting provision of services and casework, the doctors often asked the social worker for a social assessment (41 per cent of the episodes), particularly when patients presented vague psychosomatic complaints. This was understandable in view of the exploratory nature of the project. There is little doubt that the social worker's full assessment contributed towards a more comprehensive psycho-social diagnosis, particularly in the psychosomatic field. However, some doctors and social workers may question whether such a large proportion of the social worker's effort should be spent on these diagnostic functions. It is possible that the general practitioner of the future with more training in the behavioural sciences, psychiatry and community medicine may want to take on a larger share of these functions.

As the social worker did not restrict referrals to her and took on all comers, we assumed that the majority of cases would be referred after assessment to other agencies. Comparing the social worker's intention with the work she actually did, we found that she had overestimated the number of cases she would be able to refer to other social workers in the community. Over the four years she took on for casework help about 40 per cent of the episodes referred to her, in 20 per cent of the episodes her activities were mainly confined to assessment and first aid, and only 29 per cent of the episodes were referred to other agencies as a main method of disposal, though a further 15 per cent were referred after casework help in the practice. Thus a great many patients received social help as part of the team work within the practice.

It is difficult to estimate how much of the social work carried out was only acceptable within the practice setting and how many of these clients might have been transferred fairly easily to a social agency in close contact with the general practice, such as an area office of the Borough's Social Service Department. Our impression was that some early marital difficulties and adolescent problems, crises of bereavement and anxiety about retirement may not have found their way to the Social Service Department. We are also inclined to think that crises occasioned by illness and especially terminal illness at home were more easily helped in close contact with the doctor. Similar considerations apply to the recently bereaved. Patients who were chronically ill, physically or mentally, were often carried within the practice, as this seemed to be their life-line in trouble. And finally, we found that the practice social worker was often left with patients who had persistent personality problems. Not infrequently these very difficult people had exhausted and exasperated other sources of help and now only had the general practitioner and his team to whom they could turn.

Gaps in Services
The referral for social care of patients with chronic and sometimes progressive physical illness showed up gaps in services for the chronically sick and the terminally ill at home. It seemed to us that social workers were needed not only as co-ordinators of services but also as supports to those concerned with the chronically or terminally ill patients, be they family, neighbours or volunteers. The social worker and doctors also had to use imagination and practical common sense in searching out resources in the community. Many additional and comparatively simple services seemed to be required, for instance, night-sitters, extended good neighbour services and a telephone service for the disabled and housebound, jointly staffed by volunteers and patients themselves.

The social needs of patients with chronic psychiatric illness or long-standing personality disorders presented baffling problems to the practice team. Camden and its surrounding boroughs probably have the greatest concentration of psychiatrists and psychiatric out-patient clinics in Great Britain and there are many good facilities in the area. Yet, a considerable proportion of the chronically mentally ill seemed to be without appropriate help and used the general practice team as a life-line for support, particularly in crises. As we have shown, the social worker was able to help some of these patients over hurdles from time to time; but the team felt in need of regular consultative sessions with a psychiatrist, not only to define problems and diagnoses more sharply, but also to establish more appropriate ways of helping these patients and their families. We indicated when describing the nurse's treatment room that additional and different kinds of day-care facilities may be needed. There is possibly also room for more volunteer and community effort in order to support chronically maladjusted patients and their families. It seemed to us that more experimentation is required. One also hopes that the reorganisation of the personal social services into generically based area teams will not lead to a neglect of the special skills and the close collaboration with doctors and psychiatrists which will always be essential with this particularly difficult group of clients.

Some of these gaps in the care of the chronically ill and disabled, particularly of the mentally ill, raise questions about the most effective use of scarce resources, for example, in day-care for the mentally ill. Should preference be given to patients with a good prognosis, who with appropriate help might return to normal life and employment or should emphasis be placed on alleviating the continuing problems of the chronically sick? During the middle sixties the Camden Health Department had a clear policy of using scarce extra resources for those with a chance of rehabilitation. This enabled the practice team to consider alternative ways of helping chronically disabled patients. This clarity about priorities on the part of the local authority was preferable to the confusion which can arise from vague assumptions that a comprehensive service is available for everyone.

Teamwork and Mutual Learning

The general practice team, including the social worker, found that the process of mutual learning had been of central importance in the project. The presence of the social worker led to systematic attention being paid to psycho-social aspects of patient-care which are often closely interlinked with medical needs. Individual members of the team widened their concepts of their professional skills and discovered new delineations of roles; they also became more comfortable about interchange of functions. They adopted more flexible and imaginative attitudes towards the areas of client needs which are characteristically vague in primary medical care. At the same time everyone became more sharply aware of their individual skills. At the end of the project the early conflicts over rigid boundaries and functions of, say, health visitor and social worker appeared in retrospect so inappropriate that the team looked back at themselves with surprised amusement.

The project brought out clearly what the essence of productive teamwork is. First of all, it was based on a concept of partnership, equality and respect for each other's expertise and functions, and this kind of professional respect extended to all the non-medical members of the team. The creation of a regular, well-organised channel of communication made it possible to discuss problems in an orderly fashion, to forge a common language and to clarify different approaches and perceptions as an on-going process. Mutual support in face of much uncertainty and of intractable problems led to a release of purposeful energy and to an atmosphere of greater hope which possibly communicated itself to the patients and their families. Frank discussion and fruitful interaction had a cohesive and anxiety-reducing effect, yet the group was never unduly introspective but always strongly oriented towards its purposes and towards the patients and the outside world.

The doctors' expectations of the social worker's achievements were on the whole realistic and were much helped by the regular case discussions. Individual doctors approached social work differently, and the kinds of problems for which they wanted help depended on their own experience, interest and personality as well as on the patient's needs. It was noticeable that particularly those doctors who had no previous experience of social work soon learned where it could be of help, so that most of the situations they referred were appropriate and worth tackling.

We have stressed how much the social worker in interaction with her medical and nursing colleagues changed her approach to casework, especially in response to crises; how she became more decisive and active when the situation demanded it. She learned to try simple solutions first, realising for instance that progress at work or in a leisure-pursuit can have considerable repercussions on difficult personal problems and relationships. This implied that she paid more attention than she and other social workers have done in the past to the patients' version of their most vexing problems, giving up the quest for 'underlying causes' when they were not directly relevant. She learned much from the doctors' informal use of anybody in the community who could do something for the patients and found herself eagerly looking for volunteers and neighbourly helpers, particularly when patients were housebound and their relatives frail.

When evaluating the social worker's methods, we have to remind ourselves that the project involved one particular social worker and her consultative colleague and that one cannot generalise from one specific experience. We do not know how effective these flexible methods were in terms of measurable outcome. It is our impression that the social worker's predominantly short-term intervention, in the context of general practice where people can always return easily and her use of a variety of helping methods, always preceded by a thorough-going assessment, were promising.

We cannot assess with any precision how the presence of a social worker and the infusion of her particular skills into the team affected the work of the practice generally or how roles altered as a result. But we can say with certainty that the respective roles of the health visitor and the social worker became more clearly differentiated, although more could have been achieved had the arbitrary differentiation by age-groups not been so forcefully introduced at the beginning. We are also confident that the practice team became more aware of covert social pathology and how to enlist social treatment resources.

Relationships with the Social Services
We have referred a good deal to the social worker's linking and co-ordinating functions with many statutory and voluntary agencies in the community. At the beginning of the project it was noticeable how few contacts the practice team had with outside agencies, considering the large number of social needs that were detected. This was partly due to lack of knowledge about appropriate facilities and how to use them, but it was also related to some lack of confidence in outside resources arising from previous misunderstandings. For instance, doctors on the one hand and officials in the social services on the other, had different perceptions of what constituted a 'crisis'. If people who usually cope well suddenly break down or if the management of a physically or mentally ill person collapses, a general practitioner will consider this a crisis and seek a quick reaction from the social services. The social worker might find difficulty in responding instantly, even feeling that this urgent pressure was unreasonable. The practice social worker was able, by encouraging more discussion between the general practitioner and social workers in the district, to bring about a greater understanding of their respective functions and constraints. Whenever other social workers or helpers were involved

in a case it was the practice social worker's aim to further direct contact between the helpers and the doctors and to remain in the background herself, but be ready to oil the wheels if necessary.

One of the tangible results of this project is the much easier and more frequent interchange between the general practitioners and the many social services in the area. If these general practitioners were now to find themselves without an attached social worker, they would know their way about and be able to obtain appropriate social help for their patients and families, especially since the barriers of fragmentation of services have been removed.

Prevention

It has often been suggested that the attachment of a social worker to general practice could lead to the early discovery of incipient social malaise and so to the prevention of more serious social breakdown. Most of the problems dealt with in this project were serious and complex and many were of long standing. In these cases the social worker's help could not be termed preventive. However, the social worker was also in touch with some early adolescent and marital difficulties, with crises at bereavement and anxieties about retirement and these interventions may have been preventive. In addition, the social worker's accessibility, her on-going contacts with a number of vulnerable families and individuals and her chance to intervene promptly in a crisis may also have had preventive implications. But only systematic experiment could yield more precise answers to these questions.

Monitoring Social Work

This action study extended beyond the attachment of a social worker to a general practice and included the development of simple monitoring devices of her social work activities. In this the research team at the National Institute for Social Work Training played a key role. The keeping of simple, statistically analysable records enabled us to see at any point in time who the clients were, who referred them and why, what their problems were and what methods of social treatment had been used. It made it possible for us to compare the client population with the practice population and with the neighbourhood, to observe trends over time and to ask pertinent questions—for instance: why did the social worker refer fewer cases to outside agencies during the last two years of the project? In what circumstances did the doctor ask the social worker for an assessment rather than for provision of

CONCLUSIONS AND REFLECTIONS

services or casework? In what type of case did the social worker require more time for exploratory interviews?

However, the simple precoded record system we devised and the monitoring activities built on it only constitute a small beginning and much remains to be done. For example, we did not achieve a meaningful system of classifying the inter-related clusters of problems clients brought to social workers and we had to resort to the relatively unsatisfactory method of assigning one 'main' problem to each client, recording any other difficulties as 'subsidiary' problems. Similar difficulties occur in relation to medical diagnosis. Further studies are required to tackle the problems of classifying social problems and medical diagnosis in a way which is meaningful in the context of general practice.

A monitoring system of the kind we have described will be needed in the social service departments, both to inform social work practice and to help forward planning. Already we have been able to pass on to colleagues in social service departments some lessons learned in the course of this project.

The Role of the Social Worker in General Practice
What emerges about the role of a social worker in general practice?

A social worker in general practice can probably make her fullest contribution if she works in equal partnership with her medical and non-medical colleagues as a member of a team.

She contributes to a more comprehensive diagnosis by adding her knowledge about the psycho-social aspects of the patients' functioning, their relationships and the social systems in which they move.

She will be a link between the practice and the many statutory and voluntary resources which exist in order to help people with problems in living.

In her therapeutic role she will have to cope with a wide variety of situations, using a broad repertoire of helping techniques, ranging from simple information and advice through intensive crisis help to long-term casework. Not the least of her skills will consist in knowing at what point to call in more specialised help.

Finally, the social worker in general practice has an educative role within the working group; and a function as a teacher of social work theory and practice to medical, nursing and social work students.

The Future
This project has shown that one group practice in a London borough

can keep a full-time social worker—as well as others in a variety of agencies—busy in meeting serious psycho-social needs among their patients. Does it follow that all group practices should have a full-time social worker assigned to them? Not necessarily.

Some general practitioners may not wish to work in multi-professional teams. They may want to refine their medical skills rather than become involved with the social malaise of their patients. Some social service departments may consider that scarce social work resources should be deployed more, for example, in forging close links with schools rather than with general practice. Whatever the organisational decisions may be, the inter-related medical and social needs of people will remain. Whether clients have to knock at one or more doors to receive the medical and social help they need is perhaps less important than that the rooms they enter should inter-connect.

Surveys so far carried out among general practitioners (mentioned in Chapter 1) and our own experience suggest that there is ample scope for experiment with different forms of liaison between general practice and social work, including secondment and attachment of social workers to general practice. For example, part-time secondment from the area social service office may be appropriate for single-handed small group practices. These social workers could have regular consultations with general practitioners, pick up referrals at the surgery, deal with those patients who only need assessment or short-term help within the practice and link patients needing more extended help with the appropriate community resources. One could also experiment with time-limited attachments of social workers to general practices. Here the social worker would be seconded to a practice for a year or two with the specific aim of creating better channels of communication, referral and reporting back between the general practice and the personal social services of the area. By the end of the secondment the local area social service office and other agencies would have worked out appropriate methods of collaboration which may render a specific attachment of a social worker to general practice unnecessary.

We hope that in future the traffic between medicine and social work will be two-way and that general practitioners will also be frequent visitors to the area social service offices to discuss not only individual cases but issues affecting the social and medical care of the local population. Other forms of collaboration may emerge as a result of joint discussions between interested general practitioners and social service organisations in an area.

Health centres employing about a dozen general practitioners would presumably need full-time social workers. For example, Miss Neill's successor, now a staff member of the Camden Social Service Department will be attached as a full-time social worker to Camden's first Health Centre which will include the Caversham Centre, as well as another group practice. This social worker will be able to share in the resources of the Social Service Department and gain professional stimulation from contact with social work colleagues. She will be able to encourage doctors and ancillary staff to have active links with social workers in the area offices, since many patients will need specialised help and resources beyond the scope of the practice social worker. It would be a great pity if the attachment of social workers to general practice were to lead to a concept of 'my social worker' and inhibit more general and direct collaboration between general practitioners, social workers and other helpers in the community.

Another sphere of collaboration would be joint training in health centres and in large group practices for general practitioner trainees, social work and health visitor students. However, such combined training needs much thought and preparation. It must be remembered how different are the training environment, the content and methods of teaching in the three professions, how different their expectations and their image of their professional roles. It will not be sufficient, and possibly even confusing to conduct joint case discussions without considering the more basic ingredients of medico-social teaching. This thinking will have to be done not merely at field level, but among educators in central positions.

Co-operation between medicine and the helping professions built on a variety of patterns could bring about much cross-fertilisation between the professions. It would enable the general practitioners to keep in closer touch with the community services which will no longer be a set of rather inaccessible specialist services in the Town Hall, but comprehensive social services in the locality easily accessible and essential to the daily work of a 'primary' physician. Social workers, while having opportunities for working closely with colleagues in the general practice team, would be able to draw sustenance and refreshment from their own professional group. In this way each profession would be able to retain its own identity, but broader horizons would open up for professional development beyond fixed roles which can then become more attuned to the needs of the surrounding community

REFERENCES

GOLDBERG, E. M. *et al* (1970), *Helping the Aged : A Field Experiment in Social Work*. London, Allen & Unwin.

HARRIS, A. I. (1968), *Social Welfare for the Elderly, vol I.*, London, HMSO.

TUNSTALL, J. (1966), *Old and Alone*. London, Routledge & Kegan Paul.

APPENDIX A

REFERRAL NOTES TO SOCIAL WORKER

from Nurse
'Could you help this poor lady who has a degenerative condition. She is in continuous pain, and nothing seems to help. As she feels she is not getting better, she is very depressed. I see her weekly for injections, and try to give her a little support, but during the last few weeks, I have the impression she is losing the battle and giving up. (Walking stick is one thing which would help a little, can you get her one, please?).'

from the Secretary
'This is for your information only. This patient's husband went into hospital for a partial gastrectomy and was found to have an inoperable condition: prognosis very bad, so inevitably they will be needing help soon. Until then, note the names for reference.'

from the Senior Receptionist
'Mr Smith's daughter says he's extremely ill and sleeps most of the time. She can't get out—she'd like to see you.'

from the Junior Receptionist
re. Mrs G., 'I spoke to this lady while I was officiating at the reception desk, gave her your phone number. She is having trouble with her son age 20. She thinks that if she tells him she is going to come and see you this will *frighten* him into behaving.'

from the Doctors
Malcolm, 12, behaviour problem. Young boy in disturbed family situation. Truanting and stealing.

Keith, 15, big-teenage stuff—and potential problems—police already been in picture.

Raymond, 16, expelled from home by mother.

Daniel, 19, depressed boy, suicide attempt.

Jennifer, 20, university breakdown, drugs, etc.

Colin, 20, not been to work for 3 days—given cert. 'Depression'. 3 jobs in 3 months. Would like to be a journalist. Going home to Ireland for Xmas. Please sort out.

Brenda, 21, reactive depression. Love-affair problems.

Colin, 22, off work with asthma. Says he has no friends, never goes out. We know family very well.

Bill, 24, unemployed since accident 1 year ago. Qualified electrician.

Mrs A., 27, agitated depression consequent upon severe matrimonial difficulties arising from her childless marriage.

Mr E., 27, breakdown of marriage (both spouses married twice). Child at risk.

Mrs D., 28, depressed since husband out of jail.

Mrs B., 29, husband recently left home. Said to be alcoholic. Many anxiety symptoms, abdominal pain, loss of weight. 2 children. Help needed through crisis. Coming for physical examination Tuesday.

Mrs F., 29, trouble at home, even worse than usual. Tom impossible to get up in the morning. Mrs F. not sleeping. Mr F. aggressive. Mrs F. worried about reaction on daughter.

Mrs K., 33, suffering from depression. Some elements of 'captive wife' syndrome. Hasn't been out for 6 months. Can't face anyone outside the family. Visit at home in the first instance, please.

Mrs I., 35, advice needed for child, age 7, having headaches. Father in jail for 18-months sentence. Camden welfare visitor attending but can we help too?

Mrs H., 37, carcinoma of stomach. Dying at home. Support for family.

Mr G., 40, Parkinsonism. Greek Cypriot. Has ailing and neurotic wife. Supported by teenage children and social security. Has not worked since coming to this country. No social worker visiting.

Mrs B., 40, can't bear people to talk to her. Very bad tempered. Bad at work, worse at home.

Mrs A., 40, requests information on addictive drugs as she wishes to arrange a small group amongst local parents.

Mrs W., 50, 2 years widowed. Depressed? Menopausal. Hasn't worked since September 1952. Please explore. Son recently married.

Miss T., 52, prolonged grief reaction, depressed, exhausted. Requires emotional rehabilitation and return to life and work. (Diabetic—see diagnosis.)

Mr U., 54, discharged from hospital following multiple fractures resulting from road traffic accident. Rehabilitation?

Mrs V., 56, appears as unsuccessful suicide attempt, almost certainly meant to fail. Can you cope?

Mrs R., 58, widowed, elderly, lonely, recurrently depressed woman who needs preparation for her impending retirement.

Miss S., 62, recently retired (3 months ago). Previously was telephonist and theatre usherette. Never married (invalid mother died 1956). Now case of compulsive eating and rapid weight gain. Problem: adjustment to retirement.

Miss Mc., 69, lives with two maiden sisters, getting on each other's nerves.

Mr Q., 79, widower, living alone—influenza. Another poor old darling—I wish we had a 10-bedded nursing home where we could look after people like this until they were better . . . .

Mr F., 74, depressed and frightened—'life not worth living'—?? could you please ring.

Mrs U., 79, worried about Council clearance scheme, furniture, rents, etc. Will ring you.

Mrs M., 80, acute attack of bronchitis. Lives alone in basement flat and refuses admission to hospital. Not keen to have assistance at home.

Mr G., 82, wife 80, very independent, wife says they've never had anything —Xmas parcels etc. from anyone—or asked—or would dream of asking for Meals-on-Wheels—but might be persuaded in time? Would like to see you.

Mr O., 85, frail old man, partially sighted, living alone. Falling about at home. Family concerned. Please investigate possibility of admission to a home for elderly blind people.

Mrs K., 86, arthritic, old and lonely. Living in top room of tall house. Husband buried yesterday.

Mrs I., 97, has home-help, nurse twice-weekly. Daughter says 'Almost nervous wreck because Mrs. I is an old devil to her and relations and an angel to outsiders visiting'.

APPENDIX B

RECORD CARD

Date of Referral............ Referrer............ Country of Birth............ Age........ Sex........ Marital State

HOUSEHOLD COMPOSITION

Pts. not seen: Reason............

Relationship to Patient	Age	Marital State	Present/Past Employment (Incl. retired/unemployed)
A (Pt.)............			
B............			
C............			
D............			
E............			
F............			
G............			

(Ring H.O.H.)

FOR UNEMPLOYED/RETIRED PEOPLE ONLY

SOURCE OF INCOME	AMOUNT
Health Insurance............	
Retirement Pension............	
Unemployment Insurance............	
Social Security Benefit............	
Savings............	
Other............	

OTHER CASE NUMBERS

PATIENT	OTHER RELATIVES

TYPE OF HOUSING............ OWNERSHIP............ NO. OF ROOMS............

FIXED BATH............ Lack of Amenities (e.g. w c)............

ASSESSMENT: Suitable/Unsuitable/Detrimental REHOUSING: Recent change/change impending/N.A.

NAME............ ADDRESS:............ DOCTOR:............ CASE NO:............

NAME .... ADDRESS .... DOCTOR .... CASE NO ....

PRESENT MEDICAL DIAGNOSIS
_____

Problems presented by Pt. to Dr. ....

....

Problems presented by Dr. to S.W. ....

Problems presented by Pt. to S.W. ....

Other agencies involved now ....

Agencies involved in the past ....

Plan of Action at Referral: Category: ....

PROBLEMS REVEALED (*underline main problem*)

Comments: ....
....
....

Marital .... Y

Parent/Child X

Relationship in wider family group 0

Financial 1

Physical environment (e.g. housing) 2

Community Relations (e.g. social isolation) 3

Anxiety about illness 4

Personality difficulties 5

School/Vocational/Work problems 6

Need for social services arising from incapacity 7

Personal crisis (from bereavement, surgery) 8

Other (specify) 9

CLOSING SUMMARY   No. Office Interviews.................   No. Home Visits.................   Total.................

CONTACT: Patient/Relative/Social Agency

If 'SOCIAL AGENCY': letter/telephone/conference
RING SOCIAL AGENCY CONTACTED AND
RING AND UNDERLINE AGENCY TO WHICH PATIENT IS HANDED ON

Length of Contact.................

Disposal Category.................

Children's Dept.	Y
Education Dept.	X
L.A. Health Dept. (a) Physical Health	0
,, ,, (b) Mental Health	1
,, ,, ,, (c) Home Help Service	2
L.A. Welfare Dept.	3
Housing	4
Hospital MSW/PSW	5
Hospital Consultant (e.g. psychiatrist)	6
Probation Service	Y
Dpt. Employment (e.g. D.R.O.)	X
Dpt. Social Security	0
Other Statutory Depts.	1
Voluntary Social Work Agencies.	2
Other voluntary agencies (e.g. Red + & WVS.)	3
Other, miscellaneous (specify)	4

REASON FOR CLOSURE

Patient discontinued	Y
Mutual agreement	X
S.W. decision	0
Moved away	1
Died	2
Other	3

OUTCOME

S.W.'s Opinion		Patient's Opinion	
Much improved	Y	Much improved	3
Somewhat improved	X	Somewhat improved	4
No change	0	No change	5
Deterioration	1	Deterioration	6
Not ascertained	2	Not ascertained	7

Comments.................

[This is followed by space for CONTENT OF INTERVIEWS]

CODING INSTRUCTIONS

REFERRER e.g. initials of GP; Nurse; Receptionist; Outside Agency (*specify*).

AGE *actual* age last birthday.

MARITAL STATE *legally* separated/divorced.

REASONS FOR PATIENTS NOT SEEN
CATEGORIES (*code one only*)
1. Multi-problem situations; other workers actively concerned.
2. Patient needed direct referral to other agencies only.
3. Situation not suitable for social work.
4. For Old Persons' 'At Risk' Register only.
5. Patient refuses referral.
6. Patient did not keep first appointment.
7. Patient died.
8. Patient moved away/entered Part III Accommodation.
9. Other reasons (*specify*).

HOUSEHOLD COMPOSITION Household—Census definition (those eating together for at least one meal a day and/or sleep in the same room). The patient who is referred is entered first. The Head of Household is ringed (i.e. the person who pays the rent/owns the house).

EMPLOYMENT (present or past) is entered in full.

HOUSING
TYPE OF HOUSING CATEGORIES
(*code one only*)
1. Whole House
2. Self-contained flat
3. Rooms
4. Other (specify)

OWNERSHIP CATEGORIES
(*code one only*)
1. Owner Occupier
2. Local Authority
3. Privately rented (furnished)
4. Privately rented (unfurnished)

ASSESSMENT DEFINITIONS
(*code one only*)
Suitable   in relation to Patient's health and physical capacity.
Unsuitable conditions are inconvenient/uncomfortable e.g. cannot reach w c; damp; in bad repair; some overcrowding.

Detrimental conditions clearly contribute to damage to health; prevent recovery; cause a patient to be housebound. e.g. Patient housebound because of stairs; serious cold and damp; bad drains/infestation; acute over-crowding.

REHOUSING DEFINITION
(*code one only*)
        'Recent change—moved within last two years.
        'Change impending'—move expected within two years.

DOCTOR—Initials of G P with whom patient is registered.

PROBLEMS PRESENTED BY PATIENT TO DOCTOR
CATEGORIES (*code one only*)
1. Definite physical complaints.
2. Vague psychosomatic symptoms (with or without social problems).
3. Social repercussions of psychiatric illness.
4. Overt social problems only—e.g. a marital problem.
5. Other (specify).

PROBLEMS PRESENTED BY DOCTOR TO SOCIAL WORKER
CATEGORIES (*code one only*)
1. Social assessment to aid diagnosis.
2. Provision of services.
3. Casework.
4. Other (specify).

PROBLEMS PRESENTED BY PATIENT TO SOCIAL WORKER
CATEGORIES* (*code one only*)
  1. Family problems.
  2. Marital/sexual problems.
  3. Housing.
  4. Financial.
  5. Work/school.
  6. Realistic anxiety.
  7. Anxiety re own physical health/disability.
  8. Anxiety re own mental health.
  9. Loneliness.
10. Needs domiciliary services.
11. Other (specify).

PROBLEMS REVEALED
    One main problem is ringed and underlined.
    Subsidiary problems are ringed but not underlined.

* These categories were later regrouped to correspond with the categories of problems revealed. (See Record Card).

PLAN OF ACTION AT REFERRAL
is coded after the initial interview between patient and social worker (*see list below*).

DISPOSAL CATEGORY
is coded thirteen weeks after the last contact with the patient when the case is deemed to be closed (*see list below*).

CATEGORIES for PLAN OF ACTION AT REFERRAL and DISPOSAL are identical (*code one only*)

1. Information and/or advice.
2. Assessment and referral back to doctor.
3. Clarification and advice—future contact left to patient.
4. Clarification and referral to other social agencies.
5. For Old Persons' At Risk Register.
6. Exploratory interviews (a) to assess patient's motivation;
　　　　　　　　　　　　　(b) to assess community resources;
　　　　　　　　　　　　　(c) for further definition of problem.
7. Short-term help.
8. Long-term help.

INDEX

adolescent problems, 168
advice, 86, 88, 109–18
age differentiation, 56, 81–2, 95
Ambler, M. C., 23
Anderson, J. A. D., 19, 23
anxiety, 110, 116, 130
appointment systems, 44
assessment, 86, 88, 93, 109–18, 136, 140, 167
Aves, G. M., 162

Backett, E. M., 19, 23
Balint, M., 144
bereavement, 128–31, 147, 151, 157, 168
Bott, E., 144
British Medical Association Planning Unit on Primary Medical Care, 18
bronchitis, 67, 75, 143
Brown, A. C., 65
Brown, M. J., 20, 24

Camden, London Borough of, 25
Camden Council of Social Service, 148, 149, 152, 153, 156, 162
cancer, fear of, 117
captive wives, 71
case discussions, 40, 43
caseload profile, 165
casework treatment, 87
Caversham Centre, 19
Caversham project, 22, 23
children, handicapped, 27
Children's Department, 27, 92, 123, 149
chronic situations, 41
chronically sick, 168, 169
cirrhosis of the liver, 26
Citizen's Advice Bureau, 111, 148, 149, 158
City Parochial Foundation, 22
clarification, 86, 88, 93, 109–18, 136
closure, circumstances of, 102–3
coding instructions, 180
collaboration with other agencies, 146–62
Collins, J., 20, 24, 65
communications, establishing, 38
community relationship, problems in, 134
community service volunteers, 47, 160
community services and hospital, liaison between, 153

Cooper, B., 20, 21, 24, 65
Council of Social Service, 148
crises, 79, 102, 125–7, 133, 135, 142, 147, 148, 169, 170, 171
cultural problems, 119–21

death, 127, 130; see also bereavement
Department of Health and Social Security, 19
depression, 115, 116, 140
Derby scheme, 21
destitution, 118
diagnosis, and social problems, 49
information on, 49
uncertain, 139
Dickinson, K. G., 20, 24
disabled persons, 70
disablement resettlement officer, 125, 159
disabling symptoms, 74
district nurse, 161
divided loyalties, 123
doctor-patient relationship, 19
doctors, 35
patients referred back to, 114–18
requests to social worker, 68
see also general practitioner
domiciliary services, 142, 157, 161
Dongray, M., 20, 24
Draper, P. A., 23
drugs, 129, 140
Dudgeon, Y., 23

Eastwood, M. R., 24
education welfare officers, 159
elderly persons, 36, 134, 166
emotional problems, 17, 79, 117
employment, difficulties of, 159
part-time, 149
employment structure, 26
environmental problems, 83
episode, use of term, 53 n.

Fairbairn, E. M., 20, 24, 65
families, separated, 124
family problems, 77, 82, 83, 112, 121–3
family relationships, 72, 75, 79, 143, 156
Faulkner, Hugh C., 22, 49
financial help, 159

Praying

Prayers from Hymns

A collection of prayers for use with or in response to hymns

THE HYMN SOCIETY OF GREAT BRITAIN & IRELAND

Gordon Giles

First published July 2012 by the Hymn Society of Great Britain and Ireland.
ISBN: 978-1-907018-05-3

Author's Note:

Many of these prayers began life being written for the 'Hymn Meditation' published in Church Music Quarterly, *the magazine of the Royal School of Church Music (www.rscm.com); or for two of my books:* The Music of Praise *(2002) and* O Come Emmanuel *(2004), both published by the Bible Reading Fellowship (BRF). While some have been altered they are reproduced here by the kind permission of the publishers.*

Foreword

Anybody who is a regular reader of the Royal School of Church Music's periodical, *Church Music Quarterly* (now more often referred to simply as *CMQ*), will be familiar with the regular 'Hymn Meditation' contributed by Gordon Giles. These reflections are thoroughly researched, making them informative and spiritually uplifting. A particular feature of the series is that the author concludes each contribution with a self-composed prayer relating to the hymn upon which he has been reflecting.

Such a series of *CMQ* meditations over the past few years has come appropriately from the pen of a ready writer who has graduated in music, philosophy and theology. He also has had musical and liturgical responsibilities as Succentor of St. Paul's Cathedral in London over a period of five years. No one, therefore, is more qualified to be the compiler of this most useful collection of hymn-based prayers.

Consequently, it is my hope that this booklet will be widely used, not only by individuals in their own personal and private capacity but, more importantly, by clergy and other worship-leaders as a reliable resource for coordinating its contents with the corresponding hymns when frequently used in public worship.

It gives me great pleasure to commend this unique and valuable collection of prayers.

✠ *Edward Darling*
Craigavon, Co. Armagh

Introduction

St Augustine famously suggested that anyone who sings, prays twice. Many hymns are prayers. Hymns are directional: some are addressed directly to God, using the second person pronoun ('thou', 'you'), and contain often a series of petitions, thanksgivings, praises, just as, in fact, the Psalms do. Setting them to music can certainly double the impact of prayer here: it is not hard to see what Augustine meant, even if attempting to articulate what is actually *going on* when we sing 'Father, hear the prayer we offer', or 'From heav'n you came' is potentially a rather long-winded process.

Yet there are many hymns that are not prayers in their own right. Hymns that we sing in encouragement to one another ('Come let us join our cheerful songs'): these are not prayers, even if they may be sung prayerfully. Hymns directed meditatively towards ourselves, such as a setting of Psalm 23, are not addressed to the Godhead either, and so, in another sense are not, strictly, prayers.

Nevertheless, hymns are invariably sung in contexts that are prayerful: they are a vital and powerful aspect of worship. Hymn singing is worship, and so is prayer. Both are generally rooted in scripture, and a well composed or appropriately chosen prayer (in collect or other form), can complement both readings and hymns. Those choosing the content of worship events should connect all these. Sadly we encounter occasions when the person picking the hymns has not read the texts, or the preacher has not paid any attention to the chosen hymns, or the one choosing hymns makes apparently random selections. The person leading the prayers may not have looked at either. Much could be said to promote interconnectedness as a form of integrity in worship.

However, my intention in this brief volume of collects is modest, in as much as it represents but a small collection of prayers which are written in response to hymns and which might enable us to pray not so much twice as thrice! As well as providing specific resources for use with particular hymns, I hope also to inspire others to see hymnody as not only a vehicle for prayer, but also a foundation for intercession; and therefore hope that others may feel inspired to write their own 'prayers from hymns' for private or public use.

The Prayers

All for Jesus, all for Jesus

O God, who so loved the world that you sent your only Son into the world that whosoever believes in him shall not perish but have everlasting life; mercifully grant that we, walking in the way of the cross, may find it none other than the way of life and peace, for the sake of the same Jesus Christ our Lord. Amen.

©RSCM

All people that on earth do dwell

O God our creator, let all the world come before you in praise and thanksgiving, for we are your people and you are our God. You alone are good and gracious to your people, and your promises of mercy and salvation stand from one generation to another. To you be praise and glory, Father, Son and Holy Spirit, now and forever. Amen.

©BRF

Amazing grace, how sweet the sound

O God, by whose amazing grace we are created, sustained and redeemed; we give you thanks for the earthly life we enjoy, and for the privilege of being your people. Lead us in the paths of righteousness, and as we progress through life, bless us with discernment, wisdom and compassion, so that our eyes may be always open to your light, for the sake of our Saviour Jesus Christ. Amen.

©BRF

And did those feet in ancient time   (Jerusalem)

O God, whose Son walked this world, and reclaimed it for you; grant to this and every land, church and state leaders of vision and integrity, through whom your kingdom may be brought near, that as your people struggle for justice and freedom, we may all be inspired to love our neighbours as ourselves, for the sake of the same Jesus Christ our Lord. Amen.

©BRF

As with gladness, men of old

Christ the morning star, illuminate the paths of our pilgrimage so that in seeking your divine wisdom we may be rewarded by your kingly presence, revealed first at Bethlehem and still made real by your Spirit in the world today. As with gladness, many have found and followed your light over the years, lead us forward to our ultimate, heavenly destinations, where you await us with mercy and joy. For you are God incarnate, light of the world and Saviour of all, reigning in glory, now and evermore. Amen.

©RSCM

At even ere / *when* the sun was set

O Lord Jesus Christ, our suffering servant and risen Saviour, hear us and heal us as we join our prayers with all those who have cried to you for comfort and relief. As you understand our needs and our weaknesses, grant us by your mercy, release from sin and doubt until that day when we come to rest in the peace and glory of heaven. Amen.

©RSCM

At the cross her station keeping   (Stabat Mater)

O God and Father of our Lord Jesus Christ, who through Mary, caused him to be humanly born, only to die upon the cross; grant to us the grace to watch with her as we recall his passion, and the strength to respond to the sufferings of the world of which we are so well aware. This we ask for the sake of the same Jesus Christ our Saviour. Amen.

©BRF

Be still my soul: the Lord is on thy side

O God, our heavenly friend, be at the still centre of our souls, so that when we turn to you in the pain of grief or sorrow, the flurry of activity may be hushed and our worries calmed in the presence of your faithful will. Let nothing shake our confidence, nor make us deaf to hear your soothing voice as we journey onward to our promised rest in that heavenly city, where every tear shall be wiped away, and all joy restored. Amen.

©BRF

Be the God of all my Sundays

O Lord of all our days, be the God of each and every moment and place we inhabit, so that always walking hand in hand with you, we may be guided in your ways and always show forth the light of your grace, at work, at home, in church. For you reign, Father, Son and Holy Spirit, here and everywhere. Amen.

©RSCM

Be thou my vision, O Lord of my heart

O Sovereign God, the wealth of whose love is beyond all human understanding, yet whose light and warmth reach beyond the vision of our faltering sight, be the strength and salvation of our lives, be wisdom and inspiration to us, that in all we do, we may ever lift our eyes to your great glory, O King eternal, Father almighty, Ruler of all. Amen.

©BRF

Bethlehem, of noblest cities / Earth has many a noble city

O God who guided the magi by the light of a star, that they might bring gifts to the humble throne of your Son; guide us by your brightness, that through the ministry of your people, the lambent beauty of your love may be displayed to the whole world, to whom you sent the same Jesus Christ our Lord. Amen.

©BRF

Born in the night, Mary's child

Mary's child Jesus, hope of the world, light up the way of faith for all who walk in doubt, loneliness, need or darkness. As you are goodness and truth in human form, grant us to borrow from you some splinters of your compassion, that in our small and fragmented way, we may anticipate the coming of your Kingdom here on this fragile earth, for you are coming to reign, in the name of the Father and in the power of the Spirit. Amen.

©BRF

Christ is made the sure foundation

O God our Father, who hears us as we pray and gives to us all good things; bind us together in the love of Jesus Christ, the cornerstone of our life and the foundation of our faith. Pour on us the perpetual melody of your grace that we may hope for that heavenly city, where you reign, Father, Son and Holy Spirit, now and forever. Amen.

©BRF

Christ triumphant, ever reigning

Christ, triumphant through suffering, reveal your power and grace as we praise you in worship and song. Send your Spirit upon us, that in all we say or do, we may be inspired from above, and from within, by the thought of your glory, and the music of your love; for you reign at the right hand of the Father, with the Holy Spirit, ever one God, now and forever. Amen.

©RSCM

City of God, how broad and far

Father in heaven, who has prepared for us a place in the eternal City; help us to further your kingdom on earth, that in the midst of the wealth and poverty of our society, your word of truth, freedom and love may be heard far and wide, and the faith of your Church remain unharmed upon the rock of our salvation, Jesus Christ our Lord. Amen.

©BRF

Come down, O Love divine

Gracious Father, send down upon us your Holy Spirit, to inhabit our souls, that through your presence in us, our hearts may be filled with compassion, our minds with humility and our lives with the light of your divine love, revealed in Jesus Christ our Lord. Amen.

©RSCM

Come, Holy Ghost, our souls inspire   (Veni Creator)

Come, Spirit of God, and enlighten us with the fire of your love, so that we may be inspired in your service, made wise in the knowledge of your salvation, and kept safe under the shadow of your wings; for you reign with the Father and the Son, ever one God, now and forever. Amen.

©BRF

Come, O thou traveller unknown

O God, whose strength is supreme and whose name is love; guide us on our journey as we encounter danger, doubt or despair, and reveal to us your loving nature as we wrestle with the world around us. Protect us and our loved ones, that as we lamely walk in your ways, we may meet you in your crucified Son, and leap for joy at the call of your Holy Name, for the sake of the same Jesus Christ our Lord. Amen.

©BRF

Come, thou long-expected Jesus

Lord, as we wait in suspense for your return, keep us mindful of the salvation you have already brought and the resolution of sin and death that you promise. Reign in our hearts as we journey through this earthly realm, until that day when in clouds of glory you lift us to yourself in eternal glory. Amen.

©RSCM

Come, thou Redeemer of the earth

O Lord, redeemer of the earth, whose incarnation manifests the love of the Father revealed in human flesh; breathe new life into your world, that the weakness of our mortality might be invigorated by your power and glory, until that day when all nations will bow down before your throne in heaven, where you reign eternally, Father, Son and Holy Spirit. Amen.

©BRF

Come, ye thankful people, come

O God our maker, we confess our failure to share the fruit of the earth with those in need. We remember before you all those places too numerous to name where hunger and poverty are the staple diet of your people. Forgive us, O God, for thinking of ourselves more than others and for consuming too much too readily. Hear our prayers for those who work in agriculture, provide for them, as they provide for us, and unite us all in the vision of that day when you gather all your people together, free from sorrow and sin, to dwell with you, Father, Son and Holy Spirit, now and evermore. Amen.

©BRF

Dear Lord and Father of mankind

Father God, who in Jesus' tender voice calls your disciples to abandon the strivings and stresses of this noisy world; breathe your Spirit upon us, that as we turn to you in quiet praise, our lives may be beautified by your peace, and hallowed by your love. Amen.

©BRF

Ding Dong! merrily on high

Gracious Father, as heaven rings with angelic praise in celebration of the birth of your Son, our Lord Jesus Christ, may we also tell of your glory this Christmas-tide, as we sing 'Hosanna', in steeple, street or precinct; for you reign in every place, Father, Son and Holy Spirit, in triune harmony and singular unison. Amen.

©RSCM

Earth's fragile beauties we possess

Pilgrim God, you love your creation, and grieve with the brokenhearted when they cry to you in anger, pain or confusion. As in Christ you walked the way of suffering and love, hold your dear ones who cling to life, and bring comfort to all who must bear unspeakable sorrow, until that day when your Kingdom comes, on earth as it is in heaven. Amen.

©RSCM

Earth was waiting, spent and restless

O Jesus, Son of Mary, Son of David, bless us when we feel burdened with the cares of the world or pained by the hurts of others, that we may be refreshed by the mystery of your presence among us, and inspired by the renown of your cross-crowning love; for you are Son of God, and Son of Man, then, and now and forever. Amen.

©BRF

Eternal Father, strong to save

Eternal Father, we hold before you all who sail the seas. Be with them and guard them in danger, temptation and loneliness, and uphold them when sick, sad or afraid. Bless those who care for them, and guide us all to your heavenly haven, through Jesus Christ our Lord. Amen.

©BRF

Fight the good fight with all thy might

Be our guide, O Father, as we run the course of our lives, and help us to follow the path of your Son Jesus Christ, so that whether we run with confidence, or faint with fear, we may always believe and trust in him, and that by the grace of your Holy Spirit we may at the last attain the prize of everlasting life which you promise us in the same Jesus Christ our Lord. Amen.

©BRF

For all the saints, who from their labours rest

O God, who calls all your saints to witness to your love even unto persecution and death; give us grace to lead lives worthy of our calling, that we may rejoice with the saints who have gone before us to dwell with you in your heavenly Kingdom, where you reign, Father, Son and Holy Spirit, now and for ever. Amen.

©BRF

For the healing of the nations

Lord, you speak to us in every generation, and give gifts of insight and poetry to your servants, that they may proclaim your will and touch the hearts of your people. Give courage, conviction and compassion to all who hold the poor and the persecuted in their hearts, that, through their words and actions, we may all be driven to partake in the quest for justice and peace to which you call each and every one of your children. Amen.

©RSCM

From heav'n you came, helpless babe

Lord Jesus, with your wounded hands you beckon us to follow you in a life of sacrifice, suffering and service. As you chose to bear our sin through your pain, teach us to prefer the needs of others, that through our daily lives your love may be poured out and your glory unveiled. Amen.

©RSCM

Glorious things of thee are spoken

O God our rock, nourish us with the living waters of your eternal promises, and warm us with the fire of your love, so that your church may be continually blessed with your unfailing grace, and in her be found people worthy of the service to which you call her and open to the presence of your Holy Spirit. Amen.

©BRF

Good King Wenceslas looked out

Holy Jesus, as we seek always to walk in your footsteps, caring for others and blessing those who are poor in body or in spirit, guide us by the example of your saints, and in the power of your Spirit fill us with compassion and generosity; for you are our friend and master, now and always. Amen.

©BRF

Guide me, O thou great Redeemer / *Jehovah*

O God our Father, who sent bread from heaven to feed and sustain your people; continue to nourish us in our faith, that we may continually feed on Christ the bread of life, ever mindful of your saving love shown in the same Jesus Christ our Lord. Amen.

©BRF

Hail the day that sees him rise

O Jesus Christ, although you are parted from our sight, you reveal yourself to us in worship and in song. Send your Spirit upon us, that in all we say or do, we may be inspired from above, and from within, by the thought of your glory, and the music of your love, for you reign at the right hand of the Father, with the Holy Spirit, ever one God, now and forever. Amen.

©BRF

Hail to the Lord who comes

O Christ our King and Saviour, who was humbly presented in your Father's house to a waiting world; keep alive in us a welcoming heart and a burning love, so that we may live in the light of the glory of your redeeming power, revealed to all the nations in your birth, presentation, and resurrection. Amen.

©BRF

Hark! the herald-angels sing

Glory to you O Christ, our newborn King! By the light and life which you bring to reconcile sinners, be pleased to fix in us your humble home, so that we too may join the triumph of the skies, where in highest heaven you are adored by saints and angels singing your praises, this holy night and always. Amen.

©BRF

He who would valiant be / Who would true valour see

O God of our pilgrimage and master of our lives, as we seek to walk in your way and follow your paths of righteousness and truth, guide us through the dangers and difficulties that hinder us, and lead us at the end to your eternal city, where you reign, Father, Son and Holy Spirit, now and for ever. Amen.

©BRF

Holy, holy! holy! Lord God almighty

Holy God, to whom worship is due both day and night, accept our humble offerings of praise, so that our hearts may feel your fatherly love, our souls be inspired by your Holy Spirit and our minds filled with the knowledge of Christ, for you reign, in earth and sky and sea, Trinity in Unity. Amen.

©RSCM

How shall I sing that majesty

God our King, as we offer the poverty of our praise, bathe us in heavenly light and warmth, so that joined with the angels' rich harmony and timeless melody, we may worship you in sincerity and truth. Amen.

©RSCM

Jesu(s), grant me this, I pray

O Jesus, grant us, we pray, to abide always in your love, so that when tempted in this world we may be sustained by your Holy Spirit and kept from sin, and may be led to the enjoyment of your heavenly Kingdom, where you reign with the Father and the same Spirit, ever one God, Trinity in Unity, now and forever. Amen.

©BRF

Jesu, good above all other

Brother Jesus, you were born of Mary to share our hopes and bear our sorrows; guide us in all our doings and give us grace to persevere on behalf of those who endure hatred, poverty or homelessness, so that all your children may hear your word of goodness and truth, now and always. Amen.

©RSCM

Joseph was an old man   (Cherry Tree Carol)

Heavenly Father, as you sent an angel to Joseph, that his will and yours might be united, fill us with the same courage, compassion and mercy that we find in Joseph, and just as he adopted Jesus as his own, so may we be adopted as your sons and daughters, in the faith and love of Jesus Christ, your Son, our Lord. Amen.

©BRF

Just as I am, without one plea

O Lamb of God, to whom we come for healing and relief, break down the barriers of sin and division that wound your Church, and give to all your people the comfort of your grace and the power of your spirit to convince us of the breadth, length, height and depth of your everlasting love, given just for us. Amen.

©BRF

King of glory, King of peace

King of Glory, and Prince of Peace, hear us as we turn to you and accept our prayers and praises, unworthy though they be. Forgive us our sins, and heal our infirmities, so that we may be made ready to serve you daily with the cream of our lives and the love of our hearts, and by your spirit, grant us humility and patience until that day when we shall be enrolled in the court of heaven, ever dwelling with you, Father, Son and Holy Spirit. Amen.

©BRF

Let all the world in every corner sing

God our King, you let all the world sing your praise, and you are worthy of all glory and honour. By your Spirit, enable the music of our hearts to fly heavenward, that we may play even a small part in the great harmony of worship offered before your eternal throne. Amen.

Like a candle flame

God with us, God among us, God within in us, shine from our lives with the glow of joy that filled your fatherly heart when your Son came into the world. As your uncreated light took human form and shone through the eyes of the baby Jesus, shine the light of your love through the dark glass of our vision, so that your word may always be a lamp to our feet and a light to our path. Amen.

©BRF

Lo! He comes with clouds descending

Christ our true Messiah, we adore you, high on your eternal throne. Prepare us to accept that day when you claim your Kingdom for your own, when you return in glory to confound all those who think of you as nothing more than an interesting historical figure. Come as judge, redeemer and mercy-giver, so that all tears may be wiped away and all wailing turned to rapture; for you live and reign, in union with the Father and the Spirit, now and forever. Amen.

©BRF

Lord, enthroned in heavenly splendour

Lord Jesus Christ, you are present among us as bread of life when we gather at your table to give thanks and remember the sacrifice you made for our salvation once for all upon the cross. Renew us in the mystery of sacrament, the delight of fellowship and the reading of scripture, in which your glory is unveiled, risen, ascended, glorified Christ, reigning with the Father and the Spirit, now and for ever. Amen.

©RSCM

Love divine, all loves excelling

Almighty God and Father of compassion and grace, to whom we offer prayer and praise with trembling hearts; make in us a home for your salvation, that as we are changed by the glory of your perfect love, we may become temples of your spirit, dwelling in us until, in heaven, we lose ourselves in your unbounded, ceaseless kingdom, where you reign, with the Son and the same Spirit, ever one Love Divine, now and always. Amen.

©RSCM

Lullay, lulla, thou little tiny child   (Coventry Carol)

Father of the old and of the young, hear the cries of your children who wail for your mercy and judgment. Turn the hearts of the cruel and the selfish, and banish all fear of difference, race and creed from our world. Where innocence is drowned and love blackened, shed the healing light of your salvation among friends and foes alike, for we all are your sons and daughters, now and always. Amen.

©BRF

Masters in this hall

Mighty God and Father of us all, we rejoice in your salvation by which you bless the world. You look favourably on all who are impoverished in mind, body or spirit, and in your holiness you do great things for your people. Have mercy on all who fear the strength of your arm, and scatter the foolishness of pride, prejudice and power. Fill us instead with good things, according to the promises you have revealed in Jesus Christ, your Son, our Lord. Amen.

©BRF

Mine eyes have seen the glory of the coming of the Lord

O God, in whom we trust, in whom we invest our confusions and our hopes, our life and our death; hear our cries of disbelief and pain as we reflect upon the hardness of evil hearts, and the insufferable pain and shock of grief. Grant that in the midst of death, there may be life; in despair, hope; in danger, safety; in fear, assurance and in agony, comfort. This we ask for the sake of your broken, risen Son, Jesus Christ our Lord. Amen.

©BRF

My song is love unknown

O God, who revealed your unknown love in Jesus Christ, who suffered to save the world by his cross and passion; come to us in your mercy and make yourself known as our Saviour and mighty deliverer, so that we may turn from sin to love, from guilt to joy and from death to life. Grant this for the sake of our friend, the same Jesus Christ, your Son, our Lord. Amen.

©BRF

O Christ the same, through all our story's pages

O unchanging God, we bring you our thanks for your sustaining and unchanging love that you show us each and every day. Inhabit our thoughts, our prayers and our hopes; dispel the fears and worries of our hearts and soothe the sorrows of our souls. This we ask for the sake of your Son our Lord Jesus Christ, the same yesterday and today. Amen.

©BRF

O come, all ye faithful   (Adeste Fideles)

Lord Jesus, as we follow the light of your star to Bethlehem, to greet your appearing and hail your presence among us, grant us, your faithful people, so to adore and follow you, not only on this day, but all the days of our lives until we come to dwell with you, and sing your praise with choirs of angels and all the citizens of heaven. Amen.

©BRF

O come, O come, Emmanuel   (Veni Emmanuel)

O come, Emmanuel, Key of David, Root of Jesse, Dayspring on high, and reveal yourself as Lord of all nations. To you we call, Lord Jesus, whose name is above all names, rejoicing in the salvation that you have won for us by your humble birth, sacrificial death and glorious resurrection. May you reign in glory, in heaven and on earth, now and always. Amen.

©BRF

O God of Bethel, by whose hand

O God of our fathers, hear us as we remember the incidents and events of our lives which have made us what we are. Help us to examine them in your presence with humility and courage, honesty and hope, so that all that makes us what we are may be turned to the good of humankind by the transforming power of your Holy Spirit. Amen.

©BRF

O God, our help in ages past

O God, helper of all your people, support and encourage us in this life, that at our lives' end, we may be borne away in the eternal tide of your love to dwell with you in glory, for ever and ever. Amen.

©BRF

O praise ye the Lord! Praise him in the height

God in heaven, we praise you with hearts and hands and voices, in the breath of song, the plucking of strings and the blowing of brass. As all creation worships you in both song and silence, so we employ every instrument to your praise; for you are God, Father, Son and Holy Spirit, now and for ever. Amen.

O sacred head, sore wounded

O God our Father, help us to see through the agony of Jesus' suffering to the greater light of your saving love; yet make us never forget the price he paid, as we rejoice in the salvation he won for us. Amen.

©BRF

Of the Father's heart / *love* begotten   (Corde natus ex Parentis)

Creator God, Father of Jesus from before the world began, your mercy beams from on high like summer sunshine in the dark winter of our hearts. Take the imperfections of our lives and turn them to good, so that we, with all the generations of your children who have gone before us, may find your name on our lips and your love in our hearts, for you reign, Father, Son and Holy Spirit, evermore and evermore. Amen.

On Jordan's bank the Baptist's cry

Almighty God, whose servant and prophet John the Baptist was a witness to the truth as the forerunner of the salvation wrought in your Son; lead us to bear witness to the same Jesus Christ, who is the eternal light and truth, and lives and reigns with you and the Holy Spirit, now and forever. Amen.

Once in royal David's city

Father God, whose son Jesus Christ came down to earth from heaven; hear our prayers for all who are weak and helpless and by the power of your redeeming love, lead us your children to share in the gladness of that day when all tears shall be turned to smiles in your heavenly city, where with saints and angels attending, you reign in glory forever. Amen.

Onward, Christian soldiers

Christ our Royal Master, as we march onward in the way of your love, grant that we may tread in the footsteps of the saints, and come at last to the greater glory of your eternal Kingdom, where you reign with the Father and the Holy Spirit, now and forever. Amen.

People, look East. The time is near

Father God, you greet us in Christ with words and actions of love, for all the corners of the world. As we send seasonal greetings to friends and family, hear the unspoken prayers of our hearts, and bless all those to whom we write, whether they be near or far. Amen.

Praise to the Holiest in the height

O God of heaven and earth, who sent your Son Jesus Christ to rescue us from the slavery of sin; we praise your glorious name and give thanks to you for your salvation feely given. By your gift of grace, renew us daily with your generous love until that day when we too shall rise to dwell with you in heaven. Amen.

©BRF

Rock of ages, cleft for me

God of strength and comfort, hear our prayers for all who shelter from the cares and troubles of this windswept world. Give aid to the helpless, forgiveness to the penitent and comfort to the fearful. Bless the emptyhanded and restore the strength of the weak-hearted, so that we and all your children may be renewed in the healing love of Jesus Christ, our rock and our salvation. Amen.

©RSCM

Silent night! Holy night!   (Stille nacht)

Father of all, as we sing the story of incarnation, pierce the calmness of spiritual sleep with the silence that can only come from understanding. As shepherds quaked at your message of peace, birth in us a passion for your redeeming grace, that we may celebrate and share your salvation this Christmas and always. Amen.

©RSCM

Sing, my tongue, the glorious battle   (Pange Lingua)

Lord Jesus, who by your death and resurrection has won the victory over death and sin; by your mercy forgive us our sins, and keep us mindful of the long inheritance of faith in which we walk, so that we may be inspired and renewed in your service, to your honour and glory. Amen.

©BRF

Songs of thankfulness and praise

O Christ our teacher, who was made manifest to your people on earth; inspire us with the vision of your light and the sound of your clarion call, so that on that day when the sun shall be darkened and you return in glory, we may be made ready and whole to meet you, and to sing with the angels, songs of thankfulness and praise. Amen.

©BRF

Stephen, first of Christian martyrs

Dear God, who gave us the supreme gift of your Son at Christmas; help us not to lose our ability to celebrate new birth, and prevent us from becoming spiritually immune to the horror of killing, so that our lives may be real and whole, and our hearts filled with wonder and compassion, today and always. Amen.

©BRF

'Take up thy cross', the Saviour said

Lord Jesus, give us grace, we pray, to take up our cross and follow you. Give us strength to acknowledge the weight of human sin, and to lay our burdens at your feet, who died and rose again so that we might be forgiven, and dwell with you and the Holy Spirit in the glory of God the Father. Amen.

©BRF

Teach me, my God and King

O Christ our King, shine your light on our souls, that we may reflect your love. Deepen our vision that we may see you more clearly. Refine us like gold, that we may become pure in your sight. Touch our hearts and lives that we may always act for your sake; for you lived and died for us, but now reign in glory. Amen.

©BRF

The angel Gabriel from heaven came   (Gabriel's Message)

Heavenly Father, as you sent an angel to Mary bearing good news for all people, enlighten and enrich us with the good news of your love for us all; and as we are reminded of the birth of your Son Jesus Christ, come and dwell in our hearts, that we too may leap to your voice, and live our lives in the steady rhythm of mercy on which our faith is founded. This we ask through the same Jesus Christ our Saviour. Amen.

©BRF

The Church's one foundation

O God our Father, you create us, and in Christ you are the foundation of our faith. As your Spirit sustains your church in each generation, fill your people in every land and community with grace to persevere for mercy and truth so that all your church may be united in common cause for those who suffer in any way, so that laying all divisions at the foot of the cross we may come to live in mutual love and charity until your kingdom comes. Amen.

©RSCM

The Day of Resurrection

O Christ our Risen Lord, shed your resurrection-light on all your faithful people, that as we celebrate your victory over death and sin, we may be inspired to sing your praise and share the good news of redemption and of the joy that begins at Easter and which has no end. Amen.

©BRF

The day thou gavest, Lord, is ended

The day you have given us, Lord, is over, and the night draws in. We thank you that your church is ever awake, and all the world over, your people are always watching the hours with you. As dawn breaks in each corner of the world, and a new day begins, wake us all to the joys of your eternal Kingdom, so that on the last day, when heaven and earth pass away, we, with all creation shall be redeemed by your saving love. Amen.

©BRF

The head that once was crowned with thorns

O Father in heaven, who reigns in glory with the Son and the Spirit; grant to all your people the comforting touch of your healing hands, so that those who suffer here below may be joined to those who raise a shout of triumph at the victory over death won by your Son. This we ask for the sake of the same, Jesus Christ, our risen, ascended Lord. Amen.

©BRF

The twelve days of Christmas

God our Father, who sent your true love Jesus Christ to be our light and salvation; fill us with the delight of serving you and of making your ways known upon earth. As we relish the joys of companionship, and admire the world in which you have placed us, help us always to remember that you are the creator and ruler of all things in heaven and earth. Amen.

©BRF

There is a green hill far away

Lord Jesus, as we strive to walk in the way of your cross, give us grace to do your work of love, always trusting in your power to forgive and redeem us, so that on the last day we will find the gate of heaven unlocked, with you seated at the right hand of the Father, as King of eternal glory. Amen.

©RSCM

There on the hill, behold, beyond the city

Jesus, man of sorrows and risen Christ, we think we know your story so well. Carry us back to your cross, that we may see with fresh eyes your bruised and broken body and yet bear your suffering knowing you died for our redeeming. Give us pity and hope so that beyond our dreaming we may live as those who know you to be our Lord and Saviour. Amen.

©RSCM

There's a wideness in God's mercy

Father God, whose far-reaching mercy dwarfs our sin; foster in us the realization of your great love, so that no matter how battered or humiliated we are by our failings, we may always look to you, the fount of all grace and hope. Amen.

©RSCM

Thine be the glory, risen conquering Son

To you be the glory Jesus, for by your saving death and resurrection you have opened the gates of glory to all believers and reconciled the world to God the Father. By your infinite Spirit of love, renew us with your Easter joy each and every day, so that we may live in the hope and promise of eternal life that only you can bring. For you reign with the Father and the same Spirit, one God, now and for ever. Amen.

©BRF

This is the truth sent from above

O God of love, who created humanity and placed us in paradise before we were ruined by sin; do not turn us away from your presence, but show us how we must be saved by following in the way of your dear Son Jesus Christ, who was born, lived and died for us, but who reigns in glory with you and the Holy Spirit, now and for ever. Amen.

©BRF

This joyful Eastertide

Give us your Easter joy, Lord Jesus, that we may be freed to be your people in this world, and, inspired by your resurrection hope may look forward to that day when we shall sit and eat in your Kingdom. Amen.

©BRF

Thou hidden source of calm repose

Lord Jesus Christ, in whose mighty name is the source of our salvation, be our refuge and comfort in toil and pain. Grant your people healing and peace, that through weakness your power may be revealed and your love made real in heaven and on earth. Amen.

Thou / *God*, whose almighty Word

O God and Father of all light, look down on your expectant people, and give us your hope and your joy, that as we wait upon your promises, we may be bathed in the light of your love, until that day when you return in glory to make all things new and good and true in your Son, Jesus Christ our Lord. Amen.

©BRF

Wake, O wake, with tiding thrilling   (Wachet auf!)

O Lord, enlighten our waking hours, and guard us when asleep, that awake, we may be found ready and waiting for Christ, and asleep may rest in the peace of his love, until that great day when he returns in clouds of glory to lift us to your heavenly throne. Amen.

We have a gospel to proclaim

Lord Jesus, as king of all the earth you call us into the service of your gospel. As we sing your praise, give us courage to proclaim your word and tell forth the glory of your name, so that by your grace many may come to rejoice in the salvation you bring; for you reign with the Father and the Spirit, ever one God, now and for ever. Amen.

We pray for peace

Christ, our Prince of Peace, in the face of the complacency and cruelty of this tumultuous and truthless world, we pray for the communion of peace that you alone can bring. May the reality of your peace dispel injustice and prejudice and bring in your kingdom of justice, mercy, truth and love; for you are risen, alive with the Father and the Holy Spirit, reconciling the world to yourself, today and every day. Amen.

We three kings of Orient are

O King of Kings and Lord of Lords, who was born at Bethlehem and revealed to the nations as divinity enfleshed; grant us a portion of your heavenly wisdom, that we may always be guided on our journey by the light of your salvation, shining for all the world to see. Amen.

What a friend we have in Jesus

O God our refuge, we give you thanks for those whom we love, and we hold in prayer before you all those who have no friends. Help us to be servants of friendship, and give us strength to bear your love for others. Protect us in our vulnerability and keep us ever mindful of the friendship you have shown to us in the death and resurrection of Jesus Christ our Saviour. Amen.

©BRF

What child is this, who laid to rest

Christ our childlike Lord, whose name is above all names, and before whom every knee shall bow; may we grow in our understanding of the meaning of your incarnation and the power of your self-giving arrival in our fragile world. Grant us simplicity of devotion and depth of insight, so that we may never trivialise your love for us, nor lose that sense of mystery that fills and fuels our journey of faith. Amen.

©BRF

When came in flesh the incarnate Word

Lord our God, as we turn our eyes and prayers towards your incarnation among us, gladden our hearts with the news of your coming; hold our friends and families in your love, and turn any sorrow to deeper joy, in the light of the eternal promises made secure in our Lord's birth, death and resurrection, through the same, Jesus Christ our Lord. Amen.

©BRF

When I survey the wondrous cross

O Lord Jesus Christ, look upon us from your cross and have mercy on us. Forgive us our vanity, our pride and our contempt for your laws, and by your precious blood, wash away our sins, so that by the grace of your divine love our souls may be made clean and worthy of the salvation you have won for us. Amen.

©BRF

When, in our music, God is glorified

God of all creation, for whom the church, in liturgy and song, has borne faithful witness through the centuries; let us be your instruments of praise, that in us may be found that new dimension of sound which tunes our souls and bodies to the infinite beauty of your truth and the profound glory of your eternal light; for you reign, Trinity in unison, God in harmony, now and always. Amen.

When Miriam's daughters rise and sing

God of glorious gifts, who blessed our mothers and fathers in faith with the music of praise and created in us a challenging blend of freedom and control; empower us in our age to rise and sing of your ineffable love, that your people's hearts may be stirred and our ways changed. Amen.

While shepherds watched their flocks by night

Glory to you, Heavenly Father, for in Christ you have cast away our fear and by your angels have brought to us a hope of goodwill among all nations. Keep watch over us, the sheep of your pasture, and lead us into all peace until that day when with angels and archangels we will sing your praises in the highest heaven, where you reign, with the Spirit and the same Son, Jesus Christ our Lord. Amen.

©BRF

Will you come and follow me, if I but call your name? (The Summons)

Lord Christ, you know the fears of our hearts, our sins of apathy and allergy to self-revelation. Give us courage and grace to answer your personal summons to action and prayer, that we may grow in faith, feed the hungry, risk shame and court condemnation, so that through your sight and touch and sound, not only we, but the whole world may move forward in the companionship of compassion called out from your cross. Amen.

©RSCM

A Prayer by Erik Routley

God of glory, around whose eternal throne all the heavenly powers offer you ceaseless songs of praise; grant that we may overhear these songs, and with our own lips and lives interpret them to all in whose presence we play or sing; that your Church may behold the beauty of its King, and see with mortal eyes the land that is afar off, where all your promises are celebrated, and where all your love in every sight and sound is the theme of eternal rejoicing; through Jesus Christ our Lord. Amen.

A Prayer by Edward Darling, written for and used by members of the Hymn Society of Great Britain and Ireland

Eternal Lord, we praise you for the gift of music,
for the treasury you have given us of psalms and hymns and spiritual songs,
for the inspiration given to those who compose them,
for the skill and devotion of those who sing them,
for the faculties and powers which enable us to enjoy them.
Grant that, as we come together with a common interest in hymnody,
we may do all in our power to use it as a worthy vehicle of worship
within the life of today's Church and a sincere offering of
praise and thanksgiving to your honour and transcending glory;
through Jesus Christ our Lord. Amen.

A Blessing

May God the Creator inspire you;
May Christ the Redeemer liberate you;
May the Spirit the Sustainer energise you;
And may the silent music of the Holy and Undivided Trinity
bless you and fill you with love and joy and peace. Amen.

The Hymn Society of Great Britain and Ireland was founded in 1936 and has four aims:

- Encouraging study and research in hymnody
- Promoting good standards of hymn-singing
- Encouraging the discerning use of hymns and songs in worship
- Sponsoring relevant publications

The Society is non-denominational and membership is open to all. Members receive a quarterly mailing which includes the Society's Bulletin and other documents. An annual conference lasting 2-3 days is held each summer and there are links with sister societies in North America and Europe. For further details see http://www.hymnsocietygbi.org.uk/